WINTER THUNDER
RETOLD TALES

WINTER THUNDER
RETOLD TALES

Collected & Edited by
Anne M. Dunn

Illustrations by Cynthia Holmes

Holy Cow! Press • Duluth, Minnesota • 2001

ISBN 0-930100-70-0

Holy Cow! Press books are distributed to the trade by Consortium Book Sales and
Distribution, 1045 Westgate Drive, Saint Paul, Minnesota 55114. Our books are also
available through all major library distributors and jobbers, and through most small press
distributors, including Bookpeople and Small Press Distribution.
For personal orders, catalogs or other information, write to:

HOLY COW! PRESS
Post Office Box 3170
Mount Royal Station
Duluth, Minnesota 55803

To all who appreciate the power of story;
who find mystery in the common
and magic in the ordinary.

CONTENTS

I

II

INTRODUCTION

by Judy Merritt

It was a long ride to Hibbing from Wilkinson Township where I had picked up Anne Dunn, Ojibwe storyteller, good friend, and mentor. The snowy roads made the ride even longer, better. The longer it took to drive to Hibbing, the more time we had together. Trees stood guard mile after mile along the roads cutting through the northwoods. It was as though in traveling north, we were entering winter, the snow softly thickening with each mile.

After catching up on news of family and friends, and after exchanging stories of one of our favorite topics—the little people—we still had miles (and hours) to drive. As usual, I was talking faster than I was listening and began telling Anne about studying Carl Jung and the mythological approach to literature. I told her Jung believed that myths were the stories that defined the hopes and fears, values and aspirations of a people. I told her that something in the story, something mysterious and almost unexplainable, touched the listener at a collective unconscious level.

Even though the words I used were filled with explanation and defintion and didn't exactly fit the scenery or the mood it evoked, Anne quiely listened, then answered.

"That must be what my mother was talking about,"

she said, "when she told me that a story must have the strength to stand on its own."

Anne followed her statement with several moments of silence, allowing me the time to prepare myself to listen. With the snow as my witness, here is what I heard Anne say:

A skilled storyteller listens very deeply within herself to know which stories touch her in some way. A story must first have a life for the storyteller, but the strength that it needs to stand on its own comes from the listeners.

If you have a good story, Anne's grandmother told her, you will be able to gather all the listeners and hold them in your hand. Anne slowly swept the upturned palm of her right hand in a semi-circle in front of her and picked up invisible listeners with her left hand, placing them in her palm along the way. I had the sense that it was no longer Anne talking, but this giant storyteller with a palm big enough to hold an entire group of people. If that storyteller could draw enough people to listen to and know the story as deeply as she did, then it was a story to remember and to keep and to tell again and again.

"That must be what Jung meant by an archetype," Anne concluded. "It must be the stories where no listeners are left standing on the outside of the story."

Anne described the moment she knew when she had a

listener in the palm of her hand. And how important it became to her to bring each listener into the story. This process involved intense listening not only inside herself to find the story, but within the environment and the group of listeners to know which story fits the moment in which it is to be told.

All of a sudden I realized that the giant storyteller was magically scrunched in the car with us, that Anne and I were sitting in the palm of her hand along with all the listeners of all the stories that Anne has told, and the listeners of the stories that her mother and her grandmother had told before her, because these were the stories that had the life to stand on their own.

I felt then the relationship between the story, the storyteller, the giant storyteller and the listener. I felt a love for the woman sitting next to me who has taught me so much through her stories. I knew then the source of the enduring strength of those stories that live in the realm of myth.

"Trust what you feel inside," Anne said. "It is too easy to lose what you know in trying to explain or define it."

The giant woman smiled and trees nodded in snow-silent agreement.

AUTHOR'S PREFACE

My mother, Wasaygahbahwequay, also known by the colonial name of Maefred C. Arey, developed curriculum for the Indian Education Program in the Cass Lake schools for several years. Much of her work was incorporated into curriculum of the Minnesota Chippewa Tribe, too.

While preparing this collection of retold tales, I kept her precious files handy. Among the papers written in her own hand, I found this:

"The telling and hearing of legends was important in the life of every Indian. Each tribe had their own culture hero, teacher or mentor. Although all Indians were natural storytellers, it was usually the elder men and women who were the historians of the village. At that time they knew more about their tribal traditions. While family and friends were gathered around the lodge fires on long winter evenings, the elders held them spellbound with the mystery, humor and excitement of ancient tales. Story was an important part of the training of all children.

"Since the Ojibwe had no written language, tribal literature had to be handed down by telling and retelling stories. The tales were carried far. So you will find different versions of the same story. A teller would use story for moral instruction or for pure entertainment.

"Ancient stories are still told of the time when animal

fathers ruled the forest. Some tales should not be told during the summer because the keen-eared spirits are awake and do not like to hear people repeating the uncomplimentary stories that are often told about animals. If they should become angry they might harm the people by sending storms, making hunters unsuccessful, or bringing sickness to the village."

Some of the stories my mother told...I remember well. Others are already lost to me. I don't remember why the buffalo got a hump, or how a man found his woman by following a trail of fingernails along the lakeshore, or how a young woman's footsteps became moccasin flowers, or how peace came to Turtle Island. These are stories she told when I wasn't listening well enough to remember the details.

Although I have read a few stories similar to the ones she told, the new versions are different. My mother cautioned me that, "A story has spirit and that spirit must be honored by telling the story in a manner that does not degrade it." Sometimes she would say, "That story has been missionized." Nor did she appreciate what she called "the Cinderella stories" that had appeared among the people. She would tell me, "This one has been changed to appeal to European children."

When her health was very poor, she would grieve, "I don't remember the stories." As though this was her greatest loss. I have begun to feel that way, too.

Yours in the struggle . . . .

Anne Dunn

Cass Lake, November 29, 1999

I

THE FIRST TELLER

There was a time in the long ago when there were no storytellers among the first nations of Turtle Island.

But on a cold winter day a young hunter, who had been allowed to kill three partridges and four rabbits to provide much-needed food for his extended family, had a strange experience as he went along toward home.

Although the boy was quite strong, he suddenly became exhausted. Soon he was having so much difficulty lifting his feet to move forward that he decided to rest for a few minutes.

As he sat in the shelter of a great stone waiting for his strength to return, he heard a voice. The boy looked carefully about, but there was no one to be seen.

Of course, he became somewhat alarmed and stood up shouting, "Who are you? What do you want?"

The voice answered, "I am the great stone and I want to tell you a story."

When the boy looked more closely at the stone, he saw a huge face looking back at him.

Then he sat down and waited.

After a few minutes he said, "I'm ready to hear your story."

But the stone replied, "A story is a gift. If I give you a gift, you must give me a gift, too."

The boy had nothing to offer but his small game. He thought of his hungry family, sitting in the lodge, waiting for food. But the stone had asked for a gift and could not be refused. Therefore, the boy tossed a partridge and two rabbits up on top of the stone.

Then the stone told a wonderful story and soon the boy forgot that it was winter. He forgot that the snow was getting deeper and deeper in the forest, making it difficult for the hunter and the hunted. He forgot that the cold wind was driving the snow against the lodges in his village. He forgot that frost was gathering on the inside walls of his family's lodge. He forgot that their food supply was shrinking and would soon be gone. He forgot how the children would cry for food, how the mothers would weep, how the old ones would suffer. All of these things were forgotten as the boy listened to the story that the stone told.

When the story was completed, the boy thanked the stone and returned to his village.

That night he told the the story the stone had shared with him.

As his family listened they forgot that hunting had been poor that day. They forgot that the wind was howling around the lodge. They forgot that the snow was piling up outside. They forgot that many infants and elders would not live to see the new green spring. All of the things that had troubled them before were forgotten as they listened to the story that the boy told.

Afterwards they thanked the boy and went to their own lodges. Some of them discussed the wonderful story before they went to sleep. They all found themselves enjoying the best rest they'd ever had on a winter night.

Several days later the boy went hunting and took an offering of three partridges to the stone.

Then he sat down to hear another story of wonder and magic. Once more he forgot the troubles that his people were facing.

Later, he repeated the story and for a few hours, his people forgot their present difficulties and their concerns for the future.

Every few days the boy went to the stone with a gift and heard a new story which he repeated to the people.

Then one day, as the green shoots of spring were emerging, the boy went to the stone, gave his offering and sat down. But the stone did not speak.

"I have come to hear a story," the boy called.

The stone said, "You have heard all my stories. I have no more stories to tell. Furthermore, I want you to make new ones."

Then the stone encouraged the boy with a great and wonderful truth. "You are a storyteller! Where there are storytellers, there will be stories and where there are stories, there will be storytellers."

So the first stories were told by the great stone and the boy became the first storyteller among the two-legged nations of Turtle Island.

WHITE LUNG

Long ago, during a time of intense winter storms and severe blizzards, the people were dying from white lung disease.

Inhaling the icy air made them painfully sick and since they had no medicine to fight the illness, many perished.

Now, one of the elder women who had already lost her son and two grandchildren to white lung, feared that many more would die before it was over.

So the weeping woman prayed, "Oh, Creator. See how our people suffer? We are dying. We need help!"

Just then a huge wolverine entered the lodge and sat down in front of the woman. She gave him a piece of smoked duck and a cup of hot raspberry tea. Then she asked, "Are your children well?"

Wolverine burped loudly and said, "Yes, my children are quite well. However, I see that your children are suffering. Therefore, Creator has sent me to help your people. Today you must sew a ruff of wolverine fur around the hoods of your winter parkas. Ice cannot form on my ruff, so your breath will not freeze in front of your face. If you do this, and tell the people in your village to do this, no one else need die of white lung. Furthermore, those who wear my fur will become as fearless as I in defense of their family, their home and their nation."

Then Wolverine turned his face to the west, laid down and died.

Quickly the woman sprinkled tobacco over Wolverine and poured water into his mouth.

"Thank you, my fearless brother," she said. "Your good gift of fur will save my people from white lung. We will never forget what you have done."

Carefully she removed Wolverine's skin.

Carefully she cut the ruff into strips.

Carefully she sewed it to the hoods of her family's parkas.

Later, she told others what had happened and urged them to do as she had done. Many followed her wise example. Of course, some did not. So several more people died of white lung that winter.

In the spring, the elder woman received a new name and a three-day feast was given in her honor. From that day she would be known as Wolverine Woman and to this day we are still telling her story.

So it was that Wolverine gifted the people twice. First, he gave the gift of fur that saved them from white lung. His second gift was the great fearlessness with which they defended their families, their homes and their nations.

A HOME FOR SISTER MOUSE

It happened one day that little sister mouse came upon an abandoned mouse-house at the base of a tall white pine.

She went inside and discovered why no one was living there. The house was disgustingly filthy!

But it was a good house, so she began to sweep up the clutter and wash away the grime.

At last the house was very clean and she lived there for a long time. After many moons, she became an elder.

Then one day while gathering seeds for the coming winter, she came upon a homeless mother mouse with six children. Of course, Elder Mouse took them home with her.

Right from the start there were problems, and despite all her efforts, she was unable to keep her little house clean. For the mother mouse did not respect Elder Mouse and her ignorant children followed their mother's poor example.

One day Elder Mouse decided to leave. After much traveling she came upon an abandoned mouse-house. Peeking inside she found it disgustingly filthy.

"Oh," she moaned to herself, "I'm too old to start over with that kind of a mess." She hurried on, but winter found her without shelter.

Then on a frosty morning, as she sat shivering under a brittle oak leaf, she heard someone call to her. Looking up she was surprised to find that the tree was full of her relatives. She saw her mother.

"Come, Little One," her mother urged. "I have prepared a fine warm house for you. Here you will always be safe. Here you will never be hungry. Come, my busy Little One. It's time to rest."

So Elder Mouse slept under the oak leaf and woke up on the other side. It was just as she'd been told. There was no more fear and no more hunger. She was happily surrounded by those who loved her.

Furthermore, she knew that this new home could not be invaded by disrespectful mess-makers and so she was content.

SNOWBIRD AND THE WINDIGO

It had been a bitter winter for the people. In Snowbird's village they had been without food for several weeks. For awhile hunters had gone out every day, but none had returned. Now there were no hunters and the people were starving.

Mothers wept while small, hungry children whimpered for food. Older children grew weak and listless. Grandmothers crooned helplessly and the old men lamented.

"Never have we seen such hungry times," they said.

"What will we do?" Snowbird asked Grandmother as they sat together in their bark-covered lodge.

"What can we do?" Grandmother returned, staring into the flames of their small fire. "This is the work of a Windigo. If strong hunters are taken captive by him, what can a few hungry old men do?"

"The Windigo must be destroyed," the girl protested.

Looking up, Grandmother glanced quickly from side to side. "Hush!" she said sharply. Then, spreading her fingers in front of Snowbird's face, she added, "You've said too much already."

All her life Snowbird had heard stories of the giant cannibals called Windigo. Now one had come to kill her people. She knew that a twelve-year-old girl was no match for such a cruel enemy, but in the silence that followed

Grandmother's warning, Snowbird began to form a plan.

"Oh, Creator," she prayed, "grant me wisdom, courage and strength to overcome the Windigo."

Just then a loud cry from outside the lodge startled Snowbird.

"Rising Moon," someone called, "may we share your fire? I have no wood and my children are freezing."

Quickly Grandmother got up and pushed the heavy hide away from the entrance. Many Steps and her three children stood outside waiting politely for Grandmother's invitation.

"I have wood for three more sleeps, a handful of rice and one sugar cake. We welcome you to our lodge and invite you to share our food."

The grateful family stepped up to the fire and waited for Grandmother to sit down. Then Many Steps sat down and the children took places near her. Pulling their tattered robes over their heads they opened them toward the fire, gathering the small heat.

Grandmother broke the sugar cake into six portions, placed them in a wooden bowl and passed it around the fire. When the bowl returned, three pieces remained.

"Good," Grandmother said, smiling toward Snowbird, "there is enough for tomorrow. Now we shall sleep."

When Snowbird was certain that everyone was sleeping, she crept to the dark corner where Grandmother's last rawhide stood. She knew that Grandmother would want to boil the hide to make soup for her guests.

"But," Snowbird thought, carefully cutting off a large piece, "I must have some of it right now."

Finding an awl and a leather lace in Grandmother's work basket, the girl quickly fashioned a rough bag which she hoped would help her destroy the Windigo and save her people.

Then pushing the bag down inside her dress, she picked up her robe and quickly slipped out of the lodge and into the cold lonely darkness of the fear-filled night.

It wasn't hard to find the Windigo. Snowbird had gone only a short distance when she heard his stealthy step behind her. Quickly he flung her across his shoulder and carried her to his cave.

There in the darkness she renewed her vow. As the Windigo laid a new fire, Snowbird prayed again for strength and courage.

Soon the fire blazed brightly from the stone-lined pit in the center of the floor, but the presence of the Windigo filled the room with gloomy shadows.

When he stepped toward her, Snowbird shuddered involuntarily. He laughed at her fear, a deep chilling rumble of laughter that seemed to rise up out of dark caverns like a chorus of bad spirits.

Snowbird felt a scream pushing itself up out of her chest, but she remembered three starving children.

"Do you speak my language?" she heard herself asking.

"I speak all languages," he hissed.

"You seem to be quite strong," she went on. Snowbird was surprised at how calm she sounded.

"I'm stronger than anyone," he boasted. "I'm even stronger than the great white bears of the far north."

"So, you've been to the far north!" Snowbird said in amazement.

"I've been everywhere. I can run to the far north in three days without resting."

"Well, you must be a good runner."

"I'm the best runner," he bragged. "I can run faster than the spotted cats of the far south."

"You must be very brave, too."

"There is no one as brave as I am," he said loudly.

Snowbird looked at her hands and sighed. "It seems that you excel at many things."

"I can do anything," he roared.

This is what Snowbird was waiting for. She raised her chin defiantly and said, "I, too, excel at something and I have never lost a competition."

"What do you do so well?" he sneered.

"I can eat more than any three men in my village," she answered.

"Ho!" he said, striking his chest with both fists. "We will have a contest... then I will kill you."

He ordered Snowbird to prepare enough food for ten men. Then he fell to the floor and rolled from wall to wall, howling with horrible glee.

When the food was ready, the Windigo began eating greedily.

After a few bites Snowbird began dropping the food into the bag hidden under her dress.

At last the Windigo belched and peered at Snowbird. His eyes grew round with great surprise when he saw that her food was nearly gone and her stomach was terribly distended.

"You won't eat much more," he growled. "You're ready to burst now."

Snowbird was careful to place the food in her mouth while he watched.

"How can such a small girl eat so much?" he wondered out loud. "But I have never lost a competition and if you are not afraid to burst your belly... neither am I." So he went on eating.

Soon his stomach bulged horribly and he began to gasp for breath. He stared in disbelief at the girl. There is no way to tell you what she saw in his hate-filled eyes. It was like looking into the deepest pit of the black robe's hell.

Groaning in agony, the Windigo clutched at his belly and fell forward into the fire. Instantly, his body began to crumble like a rotten tree and a bloodless shriek echoed through the caverns.

Snowbird walked out of the dark cave, into the rose-gold morning of a new day and began her homeward journey.

When she arrived at the village, everyone came out to greet her. The people formed a circle around her and sang an honor song.

COLD -MAKER

One day in the long ago, Cold-Maker was sitting in his lodge beside a frozen river. His fire was almost gone, but he was too tired to gather more wood. So he sat alone and lonely. His long white hair had fallen over his unwashed face, but he could not even brush it away.

Day after day he heard nothing but the howl of winter winds sweeping across the icy land. Now he felt his end was near.

Soon his fire was no more than a single glowing ember. But he didn't care.

Suddenly he heard a shout and looked up! Someone was coming!

He became excited at the prospect of having a visitor. Quickly he washed his face and braided his hair. Then he sprinkled some kindling on the small orange ember and laid a few dry sticks in the fire pit. Soon the ember became an eager flame.

Looking out of his door he saw a good-looking young man approaching. The man walked with a quick light step. He had rosy cheeks, his eyes were bright with pleasure and he was smiling in a friendly manner. His head was encircled with a braid of sweet grass and small pale flowers rose up around him as he advanced.

Cold-Maker ran out to welcome him. "Come in! Come

in!" he said. "I'm so glad to see you. Who are you? Where do you come from? Why are you here?"

The young man replied, "I am Green Spirit."

"Oh, Green Spirit," Cold-Maker said, "let me tell you about myself. I have great power. I can perform marvelous acts of great beauty and charm. I will teach you to do this, too."

The young visitor smiled but said nothing.

Then Cold-Maker opened his medicine bundle, took out his ornately carved pipe and filled it with tobacco. He lit it with a coal from his small fire, blew the smoke into the four directions and handed the pipe to the young man.

After they had smoked together, Cold-Maker told his young visitor, "When I blow my breath, the streams stand still, the rivers freeze and the lakes are locked in ice."

Green Spirit said, "When I breathe, the streams are released, the rivers are set free, the lakes are unlocked and flowers spring up out of the earth."

"When I shake my long white hair," Cold-Maker boasted, "snow covers the ground. At my command leaves change color and fall from the trees. The birds fly to distant lands, the animals hide and the ground turns hard as flint."

"When I shake my hair, warm rain softens the soil and plants lift themselves out of the earth," Green Spirit told Cold-Maker. "My voice calls the birds back from distant lands and soon their music fills the air."

As Green Spirit spoke, the sun was climbing higher into the sky and its golden warmth fell over the land.

Now Cold-Maker was silent. He listened to the robins singing on top of his lodge. He heard the song of the blue-bird, too.

As Green Spirit watched, Cold-Maker began to weep and as his tears fell, he became smaller and smaller. Soon he turned into a vapor and was gone.

The tiny ember of his last cold fire soon burned itself away and the walls of his lodge crumbled. Then a gathering of bright clouds released the vapor of Cold-Maker in a gentle rain. Afterwards, the sun returned to warm the soil.

Around Cold-Maker's last fire, a small circle of plants sprung up and burst into flowers. Some say they were lavender liver-leaf or hepatica which are among the earliest to bloom in the northern woodlands.

So it is that every spring, Cold-Maker welcomes Green Spirit and they smoke the pipe together. Then Cold-Maker goes away and earth is filled with good, green, growing plants and herbs.

But when the stars announce the time of change, Green Spirit welcomes the return of Cold-Maker and so . . . the cycle of seasons continue.

HOW GRASSHOPPER
TRICKED A TRICKSTER

One morning Coyote got up early and went out to hunt. Soon he found four fuzzy bunnies asleep in their warm burrow. Their mother had gone to find clover and greens.

Quickly Coyote devoured the helpless little ones.

Now Grasshopper was sitting nearby and saw everything.

When Mother Rabbit returned she was horrified to discover that all her babies had been eaten by Coyote. Of course, her heart was broken and she began to weep. Her pitiful cries could be heard far away.

Coyote heard the cries and knew why Mother Rabbit grieved, but he didn't feel sorry for her.

"I must eat, too," he told himself. Then he laid down to sleep under a tree.

But Grasshopper felt sorry for Mother Rabbit and went to talk to her.

"Grandmother," he said softly, "I'm appalled at Coyote's heartless conduct."

"Yes," Mother Rabbit sobbed. "He could have left at least one baby to comfort me through this time of grief."

"We will teach him a lesson," Grasshopper said. "I already have a plan."

Rabbit was excited and wanted to help. "What can I do?"

"You must make a small flute for me to play."

So Rabbit wiped away her tears and immediately set about making a grasshopper flute. First she cut a short piece of willow with her sharp teeth, tapped the bark loose, and slipped the wood out. Then she cut four tiny finger holes in the bark. Carefully she prepared the mouth piece, adjusted a bearberry leaf over the air hole, and presented it to Grasshopper.

"This is a very fine flute," he said with sincere admiration. Then he took the flute and hopped up into a jackpine tree where he sat on a low branch.

Quickly Rabbit bounded off to hide in a shallow hole where she could watch what would happen.

Grasshopper played a beautiful melody on the flute.

"Who is playing that wonderful music?" Coyote thought. "I must find out."

So he followed the sound to the jackpine where Grasshopper played his little flute. Coyote sat down and listened.

Then Grasshopper put the flute aside and began to sing:

"No one plays the flute as well as I.
Because I am quite small,

I play the sweetest tunes.
Then I sing little songs
To charm the biggest beasts.
I sing songs of power
And my enemies are dazed.
Before they know what happened
I have control over them.
So they walk about in confusion."

"Ho! Little brother!" Coyote called. "That is a fine song. I want to sing that song, too. Will you teach me to sing it?"

"Of course, big brother," Grasshopper said.

So he sang the song again and Coyote listened carefully until he learned the words.

Then Coyote left. As he walked along he sang the song and suddenly he found himself sitting on a hill of fire ants. He howled and yowled and dragged his butt through the dirt until he'd shaken them all loose.

Afterwards, he tried to sing Grasshopper's song and found that he'd forgotten it completely. So he returned to the jackpine where Grasshopper sat playing his flute.

"Little brother," Coyote cried, "I've forgotten that wonderful song. Will you sing it for me again, please?"

"Certainly," Grasshopper said, and he did.

When Coyote was able to sing the song through without making any mistakes, he left.

As he went along he sang the song and suddenly he found that he'd stumbled into a deep pit. It took him quite some time to climb out of the hole. Then he discovered that the song had completely slipped out of his memory again.

So, Coyote returned to the jackpine where Grasshopper sat playing his flute. "Little brother," he called, "I've forgotten the wonderful song. Will you please sing it again?"

"Yes, I will," Grasshopper said. "But please try to remember the words this time."

"I don't know what's wrong with me," Coyote said, "I usually have no trouble remembering songs. But this time I will not forget."

So Grasshopper sang the song again and Coyote listened carefully.

When he thought the song was firmly set in his memory he thanked Grasshopper for being so patient and went away.

As Coyote walked along he sang Grasshopper's song. Suddenly he found himself fighting a strong current in a deep stream. He thought he would drown! But at last he dragged himself out of the water. Then the wet and bedraggled Coyote discovered that he'd forgotten the song again.

He hurried back to the jackpine where Grasshopper sat playing his flute.

"Grasshopper," Coyote shouted, "you must sing that song again!"

This time Grasshopper said, "What's wrong with you? I thought you were supposed to be a clever trickster. Why can't you remember a simple little song? Perhaps you aren't as clever as you say you are."

"You don't want to make me mad, Grasshopper," Coyote threatened. "Just sing that song again or I'll come up there and crush you to pieces with my great teeth."

"Very well!" Grasshopper said. Then he sang the song again.

When Coyote had the song memorized he walked away singing. Suddenly he found himself sprawled on his back, staring up into the sky. A stone had fallen from somewhere and hit him on the head. Of course, he found that the song was forgotten again.

As Coyote was laying on his back, Grasshopper and Mother Rabbit completed their plan by placing a stone in the jackpine. The stone had only a remote resemblance to a grasshopper. But they knew the angry Coyote would attack the stone without giving it a close appraisal.

Then the two friends hid in the nearby hole to watch what would happen next.

"Grasshopper has enchanted me with his song," Coyote thought.

He ran back to the jackpine where he saw the stone Grasshopper sitting on a low branch.

"You tricked a trickster," screamed Coyote. "You will not be forgiven."

Then the furious Coyote leaped up and caught Grasshopper between his great teeth. But Coyote could not crush Grasshopper no matter how hard he tried and soon all his teeth were broken off and lay in a heap on the ground in front of him.

The two friends sat in the hole and laughed until they cried.

Soon Mother Rabbit had another family of fuzzy little bunnies.

But Coyote was no longer a threat to the rabbit nation. So when Mother Rabbit went out in search of clover and greens she didn't worry at all about her babies. She knew they were sleeping warm and safe.

As for the toothless Coyote, he was no longer a fierce hunter, and he never sang Grasshopper songs anymore.

MUSKRAT GIVES A LESSON

A man was cooking a kettle of white fish one day, when Muskrat came along and said, "My, that is certainly a wonderful aroma coming from your cooking pot. Is it fish soup?"

The man saw Muskrat and heard the question but, ignoring his furry little brother, went on stirring his soup and feeding sticks to the fire under the pot.

"I do like fish soup," Muskrat crooned.

"Well, Muskrat," the man said, "I'm very sorry, but there's not enough soup for both of us."

"Oh, I am so very little! Surely there is enough to share with such a small brother."

"No, there is not! Now, please, go away!"

But Muskrat did not leave. Instead he sat down across from the man and watched his every move. Of course, this made the man quite uncomfortable.

"It certainly is rude of you not to offer a little food to a hungry neighbor," Muskrat scolded.

So the selfish man decided to get rid of Muskrat.

He said, "We will have a race. If you win, we will share the soup. If I win, I will eat the soup all by myself."

"Very well. But I am very much smaller than you. Therefore, I must ask for special consideration so that I might have some slight chance of winning against such an excellent runner."

"Quite right!" the man agreed, for he was a very fine runner. "In order that you have a chance of winning, I will carry a great stone on my back. We will race to that clump of tall grass near the bend in the river. The first one back wins the race. I will run on this side of the river and you will run along the opposite side."

So Muskrat tied a great stone to the man's back, then jumped into the river and quickly swam to the other side.

The man tossed a pebble into the air and when it hit the water Muskrat and the man began to run.

Soon the man could no longer see Muskrat. "I have already taken the lead," he thought.

The man was quite tired as he struggled toward the clump of tall grass, but he couldn't help smiling as he thought of that kettle of soup waiting for him at the end of the race.

At last he was back where he'd started and was surprised to see that the kettle was gone.

"Can it be that Muskrat won the race?" he wondered.

Then he knew why he hadn't seen Muskrat running along the other side of the river. "He tricked me! He didn't run at all! He swam under the water and got back before I did."

The angry man crept to the river and peering into the water called, "Little brother, surely you aren't going to eat all that soup by yourself."

Suddenly he heard Muskrat laughing above him. Looking up he saw Muskrat sitting in the tree holding the kettle between his feet. "Why should I share what is now mine with you? You didn't want to share it with me when it was yours."

But the man protested, "Oh, how can you make such an accusation? Surely you must know that I did want to share. Didn't I tie the stone to my back to give you a chance to win?"

Muskrat laughed again. "You are not only selfish and greedy, but you are a liar, too. I know your kind. You try to keep everything for yourself. You don't share with your neighbors or feed visitors who come to your lodge. Furthermore, you never wanted to share your soup with me. You proposed the race because you thought I couldn't win. But I tricked you by swimming instead of running."

"Little brother," the man whined, "we should forget our differences. We are neighbors. A good neighbor would share that kettle of fish soup."

"That is true. But the fish is gone and there's no more soup. Only bones are left."

"Please," the hungry man begged, "at least return my kettle and throw down the bones. I'll boil them again."

So Muskrat dropped the kettle and the bones down to

the stingy man who made a little fish bone soup for himself.

Now as you well know, fish bones make a very poor kind of soup, but it is just such a soup that stingy people deserve.

THE DAM

One day a certain nation of people who lived in the east of Turtle Island found that the river they relied on for water was drying up.

At first they said, "It will be all right. It's a temporary dry spell."

But soon the river became no more than a trickle and then it disappeared.

It wasn't long before the children were crying for water and the old ones were falling ill. So the people prayed for rain and a great storm followed. They filled every container they had and although they rationed it carefully, it was soon gone.

They prayed again and again, but no more rain fell.

"Something must be done," the grandmothers said.

So a man was sent up the river to find out what had happened to their water. It was a long journey and after several days he came to a village of prosperous people. He was surprised to discover that these people had stopped the river with a great dam. Behind the dam was a huge reservoir of water.

"Why have you done this?" he asked.

No one would answer.

But he repeated the question until a child crept close and whispered, "You must talk to our leader."

"Where can I find him?"

The child pointed toward a magnificent lodge that stood near the dam.

So the man hurried to the lodge where he discovered that the leader of these people was a giant toad who stood upright on thin crooked legs and walked with an ornately carved diamond willow cane. The toad looked at the man and blinked his lazy eyes. But he said nothing.

So the man spoke. "Why are you withholding water from my people? Surely you know we cannot live without water."

"What do I care?" the toad answered in a loud hoarse voice.

"Our children are dying!" cried the desperate man.

The toad smiled from ear to ear.

"We must have water. Please, have pity!" the man begged.

Suddenly the toad stepped out of the lodge and leaped to the top of the dam. Then he used his cane to dig a small hole in the dam. Soon a trickle of water was flowing down the river.

"There is your water," the toad said.

So the man returned to his village to find out that a small amount of water had trickled down the old river bed. The people rejoiced. But after a few days, the trickle was gone and the river was dry again.

Then it happened that a mysterious man arrived at their village. He came suddenly, like the wind. He appeared among them... like magic.

He was eight feet tall and wore many red feathers in his long black hair.

"I am here to help you," Red Feathers told the people. "Tell me what has happened."

So they told him how the giant toad had dammed the river and was withholding the water they needed to live.

"I will set this matter right," he promised.

Then he left.

He walked up the dry river bed until he came to the

village. Then he sat down to wait and while he waited… he sang. Soon a child crept close to get a better look at the newcomer.

"Please, get me a drink of water," Red Feathers said.

"I cannot," the child replied.

"Why not? You have more than enough."

"We cannot take water without asking the leader."

"Then go and ask him."

So the boy went and after quite a long time he returned with a small bowl of dirty water.

The man looked at the water and said, "I will see this leader for myself and he will soon be giving me more than just a little bowl of dirty water."

So he stood up and walked boldly toward the lodge.

Just as he reached the lodge, the giant toad leaped out and shouted, "What do you want?"

"Give me a drink of clean water you thing of mud!"

But the toad shook his cane in Red Feather's face and said, "Get out of here! Find water elsewhere. This water is mine."

Quickly the man grabbed the cane and stuck it into the toad's belly. Mud gushed out of the wound. At that same moment, the dam collapsed and water began rushing down the river bed.

The people of the village ran toward Red Feathers and

he prepared to defend himself. But the people did not wish to hurt him. They wanted to thank him for getting rid of their dreadful leader.

When they looked at the great toad, they found that he was no larger than a man's head. So Red Feathers picked up the toad and crushed him between his hand. Then taking the cane, he dug a deep hole and buried the toad.

From that day to this, no toad has been allowed to grow larger than a man's fist. Furthermore, they all carry the wrinkled marks that were made when Red Feathers squeezed the giant toad into a ball and buried him in the mud.

WHERE THE DOG RAN

In the long ago, two elder women were left alone. Their husbands had crossed over and they had no children to care for them.

Therefore, they made their way by fishing, snaring rabbits and grinding corn for other households in exchange for hides and meat. So they lived quite well.

But one day they awakened to find that the cornmeal they had ground the night before had been taken! They were quite alarmed to think that an enemy had been able to sneak into their wigwam and steal from them.

They knew it was the work of an enemy because there were no thieves in their village.

They became even more alarmed when they discovered the tracks of a giant dog around their wigwam.

That night they put a basket of meal outside the door and in the morning the basket was empty.

Once more they found giant dog tracks around the wigwam.

Then they called a council meeting to tell what had happened and to discuss what could be done about the giant dog who was taking their meal.

After all the people had spoken, they agreed that no one should attempt to hurt the dog for he was certainly a visitor from another world.

Then it was decided that all the people should bring

noise makers and gather at the home of the two elder women. They would set the meal outside and wait for the dog to arrive. Then they would rise up with their drums and rattles and make a great shout.

The dog would become so frightened that he'd run away and never return. Then the elder women could go on with their happy way of life.

That night, when the moon was halfway across the sky, the look-out man saw the dog coming from the east.

Oh, he was large and fearsome! His silver coat shimmered in the moonlight!

When the noise makers saw how great the dog was, they were afraid to make any noise. The dog approached the wigwam on silent feet and ate the meal in one big gulp.

Suddenly the noise makers found their courage and leaped up with a shout, pounding their drums and shaking their rattles. They encircled the huge dog.

The noise they made rolled up into the sky like summer thunder. The dog was frightened and confused. He ran around inside the circle, with all the people shouting at him.

Then he gathered all of his great strength and leaped up into the sky. The meal pouring from his mouth left a white trail across the night.

So this part of the sky became the Milky Way, and some people still point up and tell their children, "That is where the great dog ran."

THE BOY WHO COULD NOT WALK

There was once a good mother whose son couldn't walk, so she carried him everywhere. Of course, the day came when he was too big for her to carry. After that he crawled on the ground dragging his legs behind him. But while his legs were weak, his arms became quite strong.

One day the boy discovered that he could swim. In fact, no one in the village could swim better! Soon he was spending all his time in the water and rarely got out of the lake. He swam great distances and was gone for days. At first his mother worried. But eventually she realized that he didn't need her anymore and she knew that he greatly enjoyed his freedom.

Then it happened that a giant who lived in the middle of the lake stole a girl from the village and took her to his island home. Her parents were sick with grief and feared that she would be tortured and killed.

The boy who could not walk said, "I'll swim to the stone island and bring her back."

Then he began swimming across the lake. The giant didn't see him coming because the boy could dive deep and swim under water for long distances.

At last he reached the island. When the giant went to sleep, the boy called the girl and put her in the giant's canoe. Then he pushed her back to the village.

When the giant awakened, he found that the girl and his canoe were gone. He became enraged and stomped around the island screaming in an awful voice. Finally the stone island was reduced to a pile of rubble. The giant didn't like the island anymore, so he went to live somewhere else and never stole children from that village again.

The girl was so grateful to the boy for saving her from the giant, that she gave him a beautiful shell necklace. He was quite proud of the gift because it proved that he had special abilities that were valued by his community. So he wore it all the time.

Later, the parents of the girl wanted him to marry their daughter. But he said he could not.

One day he swam far out into the lake and was transformed into a large beautiful bird that is now called the loon. His loud laughter told his mother how happy he was and his songs made the children feel safe.

Then Creator made a female loon, too. Soon they had little loons and now, as you know, there are loons in many places on Turtle Island.

DEER WIFE

There was once a young man called The Lazy One. The name suited him perfectly. For when the men of his village went to hunt, he followed along looking for a place to sleep. Of course, the other men resented The Lazy One's disrespectful conduct and wished to teach him a lesson.

One day they went very far from the village to hunt and, of course, The Lazy One went along. But while the other men were hunting, he found a comfortable place and went to sleep.

When the other men returned to their meeting place, they found him sleeping. But they had been waiting for just such an opportunity to leave the lazy man behind.

When he woke up it was night, the stars were covered with clouds, and he was all alone. He knew he couldn't find his way home in the dark, so he built a fire and sat down to wait for daylight.

As he sat staring into the bright flames, he thought, "This is exactly what I deserve. I should have been hunting with the other men instead of sleeping. I don't even know how we got here. I'm probably lost. Here it is that I will starve. This has happened because I didn't help find game for my hungry people."

Suddenly a tall woman stepped into the light of The Lazy One's small fire. "Follow me," the woman said.

So he put out the fire and followed the woman to her lodge. She gave him food and took care of him.

The next day she told him how to hunt moose.

"Go wait by the lake. Sing a moose hunting song. Then blow through this birch bark horn. The moose will come."

Then she smudged him with the smoke of wild mint and sweet grass.

The Lazy One took the horn and did as the woman said. That night he returned to the lodge with the hind quarter of a moose. The woman cooked the meat and they enjoyed a fine supper.

The next day they went after the hide and the rest of the meat. The woman dried the meat and made a fine robe from the skin.

A few days after that, she said, "Go to the raspberry bushes. Sing a bear hunting song. The bear will come."

Then she smudged him with cedar and sage.

Again the man did as the woman told him.

That night they were eating bear meat.

She made a fine robe from the skin.

This went on for quite some time. Now The Lazy One had grown strong and confident. He'd filled the woman's lodge with good dried meat and many fine hides.

Now the woman called him Hunter.

"Tell me how to hunt deer," the man said one day.

"Oh, no!" the woman exclaimed. "You must never hunt deer!"

One day Hunter said he was lonely and wanted to visit his own people for awhile. So the woman guided him back to his village and left him there.

At first the other men were disappointed that he'd returned. But when they saw what a successful hunter he'd become, they welcomed him and treated him with great respect. Since he was no longer lazy, they acknowledged his new name. Then they held a feast in his honor. They danced for three days.

Some of the young women wanted to dance with Hunter, but he paid no attention to them.

Then one night he disappeared into the forest and after several sleeps was back with the woman who had taught him all about hunting. They lived happily together, and it happened that in the spring the woman gave birth to a daughter.

Oh, how he loved that little one!

But after some time the man went to visit his people again. His relatives were glad to see him and one of the unmarried women decided she would have him.

At first he refused, but his relatives convinced him that such a fine hunter should have a family of his own. He didn't want anyone to know about the woman and child who were waiting for him to return to their lodge so far away. Therefore, he said nothing about them to anyone.

So he married again and for awhile he was quite happy. But after some time he decided to return to his forest family.

When he got to the lodge he found it empty. He called again and again, but there was no answer. So, he built a small fire and sat down to wait.

"She probably doesn't want me anymore," he thought. "I shouldn't have stayed away for so long. I should have been honest, too. I should not have married the second woman without telling her the truth about my first wife and the child."

Suddenly the woman stepped into the light of Hunter's small fire. "So you have forgotten me," she said. "Well, I can no longer live with you. So you must leave now. You can hunt the bear and the moose just as before. But you must never hunt deer."

The man was ashamed, so he didn't ask to see the child.

He returned to his village wife. He began to see that she could be quite unpleasant. She sulked and pouted for the things she wanted. She went to the neighbors and complained about him. She was no longer pleased with bear and moose.

"Bring me a deer," she demanded.

"No," the man told her. "I never hunt deer."

But the woman cried and screamed. "All I want is deer!"

When she complained about him to his neighbors, they got tired of her. They went to the man's relatives and told them that they must stop the complaining woman. So his relatives told Hunter, "Go hunt a deer for your tiresome wife."

He resisted for as long as he could. Finally he went into the forest to hunt a deer. He saw a doe with a fawn, took careful aim, released the arrow and watched the fawn fall.

Suddenly his forest wife was standing beside him. "You have done what I told you never to do!" she screamed.

"Oh," the unhappy man said, "my other wife insisted and I had no peace in the lodge. I had to do it."

"Look," the woman said, pointing toward the dead fawn. "You have killed our daughter!"

Suddenly the man saw that the fawn had changed into a little girl. He was heartsick with grief.

He turned toward his wife for comfort. But she ran from him. He tried to follow her but she turned into a deer and disappeared among the cedars.

The man wrapped the child in his robe and placed her in an oak tree. For several weeks he sat under the tree, weeping.

Hunter never returned to his demanding village wife, and from that terrible day he hunted deer no more.

TEN GREEDY MEN

Ten men from a certain village took gifts and went to talk with Wanabozho about the welfare of their people.

When they arrived at his lodge, Wanabozho called from inside, "Well, Uncles, come in if you want to see me. Don't stand around outside shuffling your feet and rolling your eyes."

So the men entered the lodge. Wanabozho shook hands with them and invited them to sit down. Then there followed a long silence.

Finally a piece of wood near the door said to Wanabozho, "Why don't you speak to your Uncles? When I was a tree I spoke with my relatives."

Wanabozho replied, "I'm just thinking about the kind of customs they may have where they come from. I was asking myself how to greet them and make them feel at home."

Then after a brief silence, Wanabozho said, "You've been walking a long time. You must be hungry."

Now Wanabozho always had all the food he needed and he kept it in a large leather sack. Inside the sack were the bones of various animals.

When he reached into the sack to find something to feed his guests, he pulled out a bear's foreleg. He threw it down before the men and it became a black bear.

The bear smiled at the men and said, "Greetings, my brothers. I understand that you have been traveling a long time. I know you are hungry and I offer myself to you."

Then Wanabozho told the men to kill the bear and cook it in the big kettle they would find at their camp. So they killed the bear, dragged it to their camp and cooked enough for one meal. Then they prepared another meal and took it back to Wanabozho's lodge. They carried the kettle on a long pole and put it down in front of him.

Wanabozho's daughter lived nearby in another lodge. He'd told her to bring birch bark dishes and clam shell spoons for their visitors. When she came she wore a red sash around her small waist and large gold rings hung from her dainty ears.

After the feast, the men returned to their own camp. But the next day they went back to Wanabozho's lodge and presented the gifts they had brought.

One man said, "I have come to ask for a life that never ends."

Quickly Wanabozho grabbed the man and flung him into the corner of his lodge. When the man struck the wall he tumbled backwards and turned into a stone.

Wanabozho said, "You have asked for a long life. Now you will last as long as the earth."

"I want unfailing success and cunning," the next man

said. "So that I may never lack the things I need."

Wanabozho grabbed the man and threw him out of the lodge.

When the others looked outside they saw a fox standing there.

"Now," said Wanabozho, "You will always be successful and cunning."

Because of what they had seen, the remaining men became frightened. They decided to ask for one thing together. So they asked that they might have healing power in their medicine.

Wanabozho put some medicine in little leather bags and gave one to each man.

"Ten men came to see me," he said. "Eight will return to their homes. The other men were selfish and asked for too much. That's why they failed. But you have asked for very little and you now have the opportunity to help your people and enjoy true success. Use the medicine sparingly."

Then he touched hands with each one of the men.

"The medicine I give you will not last forever," he warned them.

"My daughter is the only one who can help you keep the power of this medicine. Unlike myself, she is entirely human and I want her to go home with you.

"Protect her until you get home. She will marry one of

you. But do not discuss this with her until you return to your village. If you do not wait, your medicine will lose its power."

So the men started home with the woman. She sat in the middle of their large canoe as they paddled across the lake.

When they reached the shore they made camp. The woman cooked for the men, but made her own camp some distance from theirs.

It happened that they made camp three times on the journey.

All went well until the last night when the men began talking among themselves about who would be her husband.

One said, "I think she should have something to say about that. She must know who she wants. I'll go talk to her."

The other men watched as he walked toward the woman's camp.

When the man arrived at the woman's camp, he asked her which one of the eight men she wanted for her husband. She said nothing. So after a few minutes of silence, the man returned to the men's camp.

Then another man said he would talk to the woman and he went out to her camp. He found her red sash tied to a tree near her campfire but she was gone.

The woman had disappeared because the men had not followed Wanabozho's instructions. She was gone, and she had taken the power of the medicine with her.

Of course, the men were quite unhappy. But the one most truly miserable was he who found her gold earrings in the bottom of his pack when he got back to his own lodge the next day.

TURD MAN

Red Legs was a strong, young warrior. Many women in his village wanted to share their lodge with him. But he had only one woman on his mind and she ignored him.

Star was exceptionally attractive and she knew it. She also knew that Red Legs loved her. So, she flirted with every man in the village except him.

One day Red Legs followed Star to the river where she often bathed or sat alone singing, for she had a lovely voice. He hid behind a great cedar and played a love song on his flute.

At last she called, "That's such a beautiful song, Red Legs. Please, play it again."

Of course, Red Legs was greatly encouraged and played the song several times before creeping quietly away. This was the first time Star had given him any reason to believe that she might be interested in him.

One night he brought a side of fresh venison to her lodge. She thanked him and followed him out into the moonlight to hold his hand and thank him for the good gift. She danced around him on her small feet and kissed him on the nose.

Red Legs went home with a pounding heart and a flushed face. He couldn't sleep. His mother worried. His father scowled.

"That vain young woman will not be a good wife for my son," his anxious mother thought.

His father was thinking, too. "Star has every man in the village after her. I wish she'd leave Red Legs alone. If he gets stuck with her, he'll never be happy."

Red Legs' parents tried to discourage the romance with prayers and stares.

Star knew they didn't like to see her with their son. She knew that they thought ill of her and she didn't like them either.

So, one day, as the young couple was walking through the village, Star stopped and began shouting at Red Legs.

"When we're married," she said in a loud shrill voice, "I hope you won't play that pitiful love song on that tired old flute you carry in your ragged bag."

Red Legs was surprised. "I thought you liked that song."

"I hope you don't try to win my affection with rotten deer meat," she went on.

"You must know I'd never do such a thing."

"I can have any man I want. So I've decided that I won't marry you, after all. I will choose a man more hand-some than you. My husband must be an exceptional flute player and a mighty hunter." Then she walked off, leaving him alone with his shock and confusion.

Of course, Red Legs was terribly humiliated by Star's loud insults. He turned from the retreating woman and walked quickly to his parent's lodge. Then he packed a bundle of food and went to a small cave far from the village, where he could consider the matter without further distractions.

Because she'd deliberately led him on and given him hope that she cared for him, he found her conduct unforgivable. Therefore, the deeply wounded young man began to plot against the beautiful woman he'd once loved.

One night he returned to the village and gathered the turds he found in the shallow pits which were used for human waste.

He carried the excrement to the cave and formed it into a man. He made him tall, slender and handsome. Then he left the turd man to cure.

Afterwards, he went to a nearby village and hired a woman to make a quilled shirt and leggings. He went to a second village and found a woman who agreed to quill an apron and a jacket for him. Then he went to a third village where a woman quilled a pair of moccasins, a pair of gloves and a fur-lined hood. During this time Red Legs carved a beautiful cedar flute and made a fine otter skin bag to carry it in.

After several more weeks had passed, Red Legs dressed

the turd man in the fine new clothes. Then he pressed a red stone into the turd man's navel and he came to life. Cautiously he sat up, rubbed his hands together and felt his beautiful face. Then he stood up and stumbled around the cave on his new legs. In a short time he was strutting about proudly.

Then Red Legs showed Turd Man how to play the flute. Soon he was able to play beautifully and one frosty evening they returned to Red Legs' village.

When Star saw the two young men arrive together, she asked Red Legs, "Who's your good-looking friend?"

"Sleeping Bear," he replied. Then he brushed past her and walked away without another word.

Of course, Star thought Red Legs was jealous and she began flirting with Sleeping Bear in a most outrageous manner. Then she followed him through the village to Red Leg's lodge.

When the door flap was closed against her, she returned to her own lodge to dream of the handsome young stranger.

Inside Red Leg's lodge one of the children said, "Phew! Someone stepped in poop and carried it in on their moccasin."

Everyone looked at Sleeping Bear. He was so embarrassed by his unpleasant odor that he excused himself and went outside. He sat behind the lodge and played the flute.

Star heard the beautiful music floating through the darkness. Of course, she imagined it was a love song he played only for her.

Sleeping Bear slept on the ground behind the lodge that night. Several of the village dogs came and laid down with him. He was grateful for their warmth.

The next day Star, dressed in her finest outfit, went to Red Legs' lodge and asked to see Sleeping Bear.

She was surprised to hear that he was sleeping behind the lodge. Quickly she went around and found him cuddled up with several dogs. She chased the dogs away and shook Sleeping Bear until he woke up.

"Because of my beauty," she told the young man, "many men desire that I share my lodge with them. But I have chosen you. We will be married tomorrow."

Without waiting for a response she hurried away.

Later that day she told her mother to prepare a marriage feast.

Then Star built a new lodge nearby.

After they were married, Sleeping Bear refused to enter Star's lodge because he knew that if he sat in the warmth with her, he'd begin to stink.

"She'll complain," he worried, "and I'll be embarrassed."

At first Star was amused. "Don't be shy," she teased.

She tugged on his arms and tickled him. But he would not let himself be taken into the lodge.

Star was humiliated because everyone was laughing at her.

"Come inside now!" she screamed at her reluctant husband. "If you don't do as I say, I'll get my brothers to whip you, and in the morning I'll send you back to Red Legs' lodge. You'll be laughed at for the rest of your life."

Sleeping Bear said nothing. He simply turned and hurried away from his beautiful wife.

Star ran after him begging him to return. "Please, come back," she wept. "I'm sorry! I love you too much to let my brothers hurt you. I only said that to make you come into the lodge."

But Sleeping Bear kept walking. He went out of the village and into the forest.

His wife followed.

He walked up a stony hill.

She followed.

Sleeping Bear walked much faster than Star and soon she was left far behind.

It was getting dark when she stumbled over something. She reached down and found her husband's glove. It was full of turds. She couldn't understand how excrement got into the glove but she shook it out and wiped the glove clean. Then she stuffed it with grass and carried it along.

Then she stumbled over the other glove. It was full of turds, too.

"Why would anyone put turds in my husband's gloves?" she wondered as she shook the excrement out, stuffed the second glove with grass and carried it along.

Not far from there she found one of his moccasins full of turds. A little beyond that place, she found the other moccasin full of turds. She was baffled. But she cleaned them carefully, filled them with grass and carried them long.

"When I catch up to my husband I'll return them," she decided. "I know he'll appreciate my thoughtfulness and he'll probably forgive me, too."

At the top of the hill she found his leggings. A few feet down the other side, she found his apron and jacket. They were smeared with human waste. She scraped the garments clean, rolled them into a bundle with the other clothing and carried it along.

At last she found the fur-lined hood with Turd Man's beautiful face smiling up at her in the moonlight.

Star screamed, dropped the bundle of fine clothes and ran back toward the village.

When she returned to her lodge she went inside and refused to come out. She remained in seclusion for a long, long time. Every night her mother brought food and placed it beside the door. In the morning the food was gone.

Red Legs went off to live with his father's relatives in a distant village where he soon found a good wife.

When Star finally left her lodge, she'd been transformed into a patient, considerate, respectful young woman.

Later she became the wife of a good man and raised three respectful daughters.

HOW RABBIT WON THE RACE

On a summer day long ago, Coyote came along and found Rabbit sitting in front of his house in deep and quiet thought.

"What are you thinking about, friend Rabbit?" Coyote asked.

"Oh, friend Coyote, you surprised me!" exclaimed Rabbit. "I am wondering why it is that some animals have big bushy tails, like yours, while others have scarcely any tail at all, like mine. Perhaps if I had a tail as beautiful as yours, I could run straight and not hop this way and that."

Coyote was quite flattered at the attention his fine tail was receiving and turned slightly to glance over his shoulder. "It is true," he said, "that I am a fleet runner, while you hop along like a frightened bird."

"All the same," said Rabbit, "I'd like to challenge you to a race. Races are such fun. Come, let us run to the four corners of Turtle Island and see who will win!"

Coyote knew he could run faster than Rabbit.

"Very well," he said. "In four days we shall have a race, and whoever comes in first may kill and eat the one who comes in last."

Rabbit had not expected Coyote to make such a terrible threat, so after Coyote went running off, Rabbit went to speak with an elder. Old Long Ears helped devise a plan to save Rabbit's life. Then Rabbit went to talk with his other relatives. He told them about the race and the plan to save his life. The other rabbits agreed to help their brother and soon runners were on their way to the four corners of Turtle Island.

On the fourth day, Coyote arrived at Rabbit's house and threw down his fine red blanket.

"What is the point of such a long run," he said in a loud voice, "when it is certain that I will come in first? Perhaps I should eat you now before we get tired."

Rabbit rushed out and threw down his blanket, too.

"Now!" he shouted. "We will have this race. If you want to talk, we can do that later. If you want to eat, that can be done later, too. Come, we shall run to the four corners of Turtle Island. I shall have to run underground for, as you know, that is easier for me."

Coyote knew no such thing, but did not want to appear ignorant. So he said, "It is all agreed."

When they were ready, they stood side by side. Then with a great shout, they started. Coyote burst into a quick lead. Rabbit jumped into a hole and disappeared.

For several days Coyote kept running toward the east and saw nothing of Rabbit. But just as he came to the most eastern point of Turtle Island and was turning to run north, Coyote nearly stumbled over Rabbit, who jumped out of a hole right under Coyote's nose. Quickly Coyote regained his footing and burst forward again.

"Ho!" Rabbit shouted, "we are well-matched." Then he ducked back into the hole and was gone.

"I wish I could run underground," thought Coyote. "Surely it must be easier. For I have been running as fast as I can, yet Rabbit nearly got here before I did."

Coyote did not know that Rabbit's brothers, who looked a great deal like him, were helping him. They were waiting at the four corners, ready to leap out when Coyote came running near.

So Coyote went on running and after many days he came to the north. But just as he was turning west, Rabbit sprang up from a hole some distance ahead of him.

"Ho!" shouted Rabbit, "I am gaining!"

Then he ducked back into the hole, wriggled his tail and disappeared.

Coyote's heart was heavy but he ran even harder than before. Nevertheless, when he came to the west, Rabbit was far ahead.

He leaped up and shouted, "Ho, friend Coyote, I am going to win!"

When Coyote came to the south he saw Rabbit very far ahead. At last he returned to the starting point, where he saw Rabbit sitting at the entrance of his home.

"I have been waiting for you for quite some time," Rabbit said. "I have been thinking that your big tail does not make you a better runner after all. Now, come over here. It's time for me to eat you."

But the terrified Coyote screamed and ran away.

Rabbits all over Turtle Island still talk about that race and they laugh at the trick they played on that poor old Coyote. Then they look over their shoulders, wriggle their short tails, and laugh again.

MORNING STAR WOMAN

I t happened long ago that a certain family lived in a small northern village. The father was an excellent hunter and told wonderful stories. The mother wove beautiful mats and sang powerful songs. So they were both good teachers for their two young children.

Then one day a terrible thing happened. The parents fell ill with a strange disease and died quite suddenly, leaving the children alone.

But the two young ones had been well-trained and were able to take care of themselves. So they never needed anyone else and lived together happily for several years.

As the girl grew to womanhood, she became quite attractive and one of the men in the village decided that he wanted her to be his wife. He sent his friend Coyote to speak to the woman and her brother.

The woman said, "I have lived happily with my brother for many years and am quite satisfied with my life. I have no desire to become the wife of any man, thank you."

But the brother recognized the nature of Coyote and felt that his sister had been dishonored. "I cannot respect a man who would allow himself to be represented by Coyote," he said.

Therefore, Coyote's pride was injured.

So he went back to his friend and lied, "The woman doesn't want you, and her brother said he will not see his sister married to a fool like you."

Of course, the man was hurt by the rejection and angered by the insults. So he shouted, "If he will not give her, and she will not have me . . . then I will take her!"

So the man spoke to several of his friends about what had happened. With every telling the tale became more painful and more ugly. Therefore, some of his friends agreed to help him take revenge on the brother and sister.

On the appointed night, they crept near the woman's lodge and one of them cried like a wolf pup.

"Go out and find that pup," the woman told her brother. "Perhaps it's hungry."

The man smiled at his sister's kindness as she put a few scraps of meat on a birch bark tray and placed it in his hand. Then he went out to feed the unfortunate little one.

But after he'd followed the sound of the whimpering pup for some distance, he realized that it was a trick to lure him away.

Quickly he ran back to find the lodge in violent disarray and his good sister gone.

He grabbed a torch and followed the tracks away from the village. Although he could see that several men were involved in the kidnapping, there was no time to get help. So he went after them alone.

At last he came upon the camp of the lawless men and saw his sister tied to a tree. Fearlessly he ran to her, cut the ropes and carried her away.

But the rejected suitor and his violent friends had expected the man to attempt the rescue of his sister. They had tied her to the tree to lure him into range.

They had him where they wanted him. So they began shooting arrows at the brave man.

After he'd been injured several times, he put his sister down. Then he fell to the ground, bleeding and dying.

His sister screamed and threw herself upon him. Then she began to weep and sing. Creator listened to the woman's song of love and grief, and was moved to intervene.

Suddenly the dying man got to his feet, leaped into the western sky and was transformed into a star. So he became Evening Star Man.

Now the woman was alone and undefended. But she went on singing. Then Creator intervened again. This time Creator lifted the woman into the eastern sky and changed her into a star, too. So she became Morning Star Woman.

The rejected suitor and his violent friends became so frightened that they ran blindly into the forest, became hopelessly confused and were never seen again.

When Evening Star Man remembers how his gentle sister was abused, he becomes quite angry and strikes the earth...causing it to shudder and shake. Sometimes he strikes the earth so violently that it quakes and breaks!

WOMAN LAKE LEGEND

There was once a man who had two wives. Although they were twin sisters, they shared very few characteristics and had little in common. One was tall, one was short. One was plump, one was thin. One was quiet, one was loud. One was rude, one was kind. One was energetic, and one tired easily.

One wife was called Weasel, the other was Beaver. They had been well-named, for they were quite like the animals whose names they'd received at their naming ceremonies.

Weasel was quick-tempered and anxious, while Beaver was placid and gentle.

Weasel often accused their husband of loving Beaver more than he loved her. While it was true that the man did prefer the companionship of Beaver, his love for the women was equal. He tried not to favor Beaver, but Weasel became angry anyway. This made life difficult for everyone.

It happened one day that the man went out to hunt and saw two otters playing on the river bank. "I'll take two otters home today," he thought. "One for each of the women."

Creeping close, he killed one with an arrow, while the other escaped into the water. The man searched all day for the other otter. At last, he returned home with only one.

He gave the otter to Beaver and told Weasel what had happened. Of course, she didn't believe him.

"You brought an otter for Beaver. But for me you have only excuses!" she screamed.

The following day the man returned to the river to look for the otter again. But he did not find it. When he came home empty-handed, Weasel lashed out at him. "What! No gift for your beloved Beaver?"

Beaver said nothing but sat on her mat scraping the otter hide. She thought perhaps she would tan the hide and gift it to Weasel after their next moon.

Every day the poor man went out to search for another otter so that Weasel would stop quarreling with him.

But every day he returned with nothing.

One day Weasel told Beaver, "I can't stand this any longer. I cannot live in the same lodge with you. I want our husband for myself. You must leave!"

Beaver did not argue, she simply refused to go away. "This is my home, too," she reminded her sister.

"Then we must have contest," Weasel said. "We will swim around the small lake near our village. We will stay in the water until one of us drowns. The one who survives will have our husband to herself."

Beaver did not want to do this, but Weasel insisted.

Weasel ran to the lake, stripped and jumped in. Reluctantly, Beaver followed.

Around and around they swam. Each time Weasel passed Beaver, she shouted, "I hate you!"

Beaver was weeping as she swam. She did not want to live in the unhappy lodge. Nor did she want anyone to drown. So she decided that she would leave and allow Weasel to have her way.

Beaver crawled up on the shore. She sat for several minutes to catch her breath, then she walked home to pack her belongings. When all was ready, she sat down to wait for Weasel. Soon it was nearly dark and still Weasel had not returned.

"She probably went to hide in the woods," Beaver told

herself. "I will prepare a meal for our husband before I leave."

Later, when the man came home, Beaver told him everything. While he was heartsick that his gentle wife was leaving, he allowed her to make that choice.

"You must do what you must do," he told her.

It was quite dark when they decided to look for Weasel. They searched all night but did not find her. Several days later some elder women found her body in their fishing nets.

So Beaver and her husband lived a peaceful life together and the people named the lake, Jealous Woman Waters. The man called it Beaver Woman Lake in honor of his gracious wife. Today it is called Woman Lake, but almost everyone has forgotten why.

HUNTER

Long ago there was an outstanding hunter. No matter the season or the weather, he always returned from the hunt with game.

Then it was that he became great with pride and was often heard boasting of his abilities and belittling those who had experienced little or no success.

He was also quite selfish. He thought only of himself and his own household, ignoring the hungry people around him.

One day as the men were preparing to leave for a hunt, he shouted, "I will certainly return with a great deer, or a moose, or even a bear. Perhaps you other men would like me to show you how to hunt. It's doubtful that any of you will ever surpass me, but your families would be thankful for more than an occasional rabbit and a few skinny partridges."

So . . . he ridiculed his neighbors.

Indeed, it was Creator who had blessed the man with such great skill. But now Creator decided it was time to teach this man an important lesson. Therefore, when the man went out to hunt that day, he did not see any game. He did not even find any animal tracks. It seemed the game had disappeared.

Then as the sun began to set, he realized that he would not return to his village with a deer, a moose, or a bear, so he decided to settle for a few rabbits. But not even a rabbit crossed his path that day.

The man remembered his loud boasting and couldn't face the other men. So he made camp and spent the night alone in the forest.

The next day he hunted again. Once more, he had no success. So he decided to spend another night in the forest and get up early to start hunting the next day.

"Surely tomorrow I'll have better luck," he thought.

When he awakened in the morning he was surprised to find an elder woman sitting nearby.

"Good morning, my son," she greeted him. "I see you have not had luck hunting for several days. Of course, you must be too ashamed to go home now. I'm sure you're quite hungry, too. Follow me and I will take you to my lodge where I have plenty of food."

So the man got up quickly and followed her.

They went a great distance and the man became quite tired, but the elder woman walked quickly and was soon far ahead of him.

At last he called to her, "Grandmother, I think we should stop here so you can rest for awhile."

"Why?" the woman replied. "I'm not tired."

So the man admitted that he was quite exhausted. "I cannot go on."

While they sat resting, the woman seemed to be staring at him. He was quite uncomfortable and asked, "Why do you look at me with such hard eyes?"

"I was wondering what kind of a man fills his belly every day and has no pity for his hungry neighbors."

The man didn't like to hear that, but he said nothing and soon they were on their way again.

At last they reached the woman's lodge.

The man was surprised to find that the woman lived alone. He wondered who hunted for her as she was an old woman and didn't carry a weapon.

"Sit down," the woman said when they got inside the lodge. She quickly built a fire.

The man looked around. He saw no food in the lodge and had not seen a store house when they arrived. So he wondered where she would get the food she'd promised to give him.

Soon the woman sat down across from him and took three small cooking pots from her belt-bag. She filled them with water and put them near the fire. When the water was steaming, she took a kernel of rice from the bag and put it into the first pot. Then she reached into the bag again and took out a small piece of dried fish which she put in the second pot. Then she took out a mint leaf and put in the third pot.

When the rice was cooked, she gave the tiny pot to him and said, "Eat."

"Oh, no," the man said. "I can't take your last kernel of rice."

The woman laughed. "Take it," she said. "There will be plenty left for me."

So the man took the kernel of rice and placed it on his tongue. Carefully he bit into it. Oh, it was delicious. He wished there was more.

How surprised he was when he looked into the pot and saw another rice kernel waiting for him. Carefully he ate that one, too. Then another appeared. And so it went...until he was filled.

Then she gave him the fish. No matter how much he ate, there was always more. The same thing happened with the mint tea. The tiny pot was always full.

At last the woman asked, "Have you had enough, my son?"

"Yes," the man whispered.

Afterwards she gave the man a long look and said, "When you share what you have, you will find there is always enough."

Suddenly the man was waking up in his camp. After a few minutes, a deer walked up to him and the man shot it with an arrow. The deer fell down and died.

So the man returned to his village with a big deer, which he shared with his neighbors.

GRANDMOTHER SKY WEAVERS

t happened one day that an elder woman was getting ready to go to the other side and she was concerned that she might find herself with nothing to do when she went across.

"After all," she thought, "I'm old. I'm not strong. There are times when I feel quite useless."

So it was that when she went to sleep on this side and awakened on the other, Creator was waiting for her.

"Daughter," Creator called. "I'm glad to see you here. Come, sit with me. There are a few things I want to know."

So the woman made herself comfortable and waited for Creator to continue.

"Daughter," Creator asked, "did you enjoy your journey?"

"Oh, yes! I certainly did."

"Were you kind to your relatives?"

The woman considered this question for quite some time. Then she said, "I tried to be kind to my relatives, but there were times when I failed. I'm sorry to disappoint you."

Then Creator asked if there was anything she wanted to know.

"Yes," the woman began, "I have always been a hard worker. Now I have become concerned that there will be little for me to do here. When I was upon my earth journey,

I found that I greatly enjoyed weaving. I became quite good at this and would like to continue my craft here. Is it possible?"

Creator was delighted. "Daughter, your words make me glad! In this place we need good weavers! Come, I will show you where you may continue your craft."

Suddenly the woman found herself at the edge of the sky.

She saw many women seated along the horizon. So she sat down with them.

Turning to the woman on her left, she asked, "What am I to do?"

The woman smiled at the newcomer and told her, "We are the Grandmother Sky Weavers. We are weaving the night into day. Every day we give color to the sunrise. Every night we give color to the sunset."

Happily the woman picked up her shuttle and her yarn, and began weaving the sunrise. As she worked...she sang the weaving song she'd learned from her mother. Suddenly she heard someone singing along with her.

Looking to her right she saw her mother and beyond her mother...she saw her grandmother. They were young and strong and beautiful.

They dropped their shuttles to enjoy a long embrace and wept joyfully into each other's hair. Then they went on weaving and singing together as a great bright sunrise glowed in the east and spread itself across the sky.

When we see sunrise and sunset color the horizon, we should thank the Grandmother Sky Weavers for bringing such beauty to our daily lives.

II

HOW BEAR LOST HIS TAIL

There was a time when brother Bear had a nice long tail. This is the story of how he lost it.

In the moon when the wild geese fly south, North Wind blew his frosty breath upon the earth and the green nations turned brown.

Each morning and evening the creek was puckered with ice, but it thawed during the afternoon.

Then it was that Bear came out of his den to look for something more that he could eat before he went to sleep for the long winter. As he went along, he met Fox who was carrying a big mess of catfish and carp.

Bear's mouth began to water when he saw those fish.

"Where did you get that nice mess of fish?" he asked.

"In the creek."

"Please, tell me how so I can catch some, too."

"Well, the creek is thawed now, so if you sit on the bank and hang your tail in the water, the fish will nibble at it. You can feel the number of nibbles and if you draw it out real fast, you will have a fine mess for your supper tonight."

Bear thanked Fox and hurried down to the creek and let his long tail hang in the water. His stomach growled with hunger and he thought only of the fine mess of fish he would have for supper.

He felt the nibbles on his tail but he wouldn't draw it

out until he was sure that he had a whole mess of fish hanging on to it. Toward evening it began to really hurt.

He thought, "Oh, boy! I sure am getting a lot of nibbles. I will have a real feast tonight!"

So he sat there longer and the pains were like sharp arrows pricking him. At last he couldn't stand it any longer.

He tried to flip the fish out onto the bank, but nothing happened. He was stuck in the ice!

Bear was frightened because he knew that he had sat there too long. He was frozen into the ice.

The sun had gone down and it was getting colder. He didn't want to sit there all night, so he pulled real hard and he was free.

But he'd left his nice, long tail in the ice. Now all bears have short tails.

He went to his den hungry and cold and hurting where his tail used to be.

He knew this wouldn't have happened if he hadn't been so greedy for those fish. But he probably dreamed about them all winter, because bears still love fish.

HEART BERRIES

I t happened that a man and woman loved one another and wanted to be together forever.

At first all went well. Then the man grew discontent with the woman. He became critical and unreasonable.

"I don't like the way you cook," he complained. "I don't like the way you laugh, and you talk too much."

Of course, she didn't like being treated with contempt, so she decided to leave.

"I'm returning to my mother's lodge," she told him one day.

"Good!" he shouted.

So she packed her basket and left.

He didn't say good-bye and she never looked back.

During the first day of her absence the man was angry.

"She left me," he thought. "Walked right out! Took all her stuff, too. Well, I don't care. I'm better off without her."

On the second day he felt sorry for himself.

"Now what will I do? I'm all alone. I don't have a cook... no one to mend my clothes... no one to keep me warm."

On the third day he was sorry.

"What have I done! I forced her out. I was critical, unreasonable and unkind. I deserve to be alone. But I'm sorry for the way I treated her. I want to be forgiven. I'll go after her. I'll beg her to come back. But she's been walking for three days. I won't be able to catch her before she reaches her mother's lodge. If she gets to her family they won't let her come back with me. I have to catch up with her soon!"

So immediately the man packed a bag of food and started walking in the direction his wife had gone.

Creator had heard the pitiful man crying and looked into his heart. Creator saw that the man was truly sorry. He had changed his mind completely and loved the woman more than ever.

"I will help this pathetic man," Creator decided.

So Creator caused a great field of flowers to grow up before the woman. Many of the flowers had never been seen on Turtle Island. The woman was amazed at their beauty and stopped to admire them. She smelled their sweetness and gathered enough to braid into her hair. Then she picked up her basket and went on.

The flowers did not stop her, but they slowed her down. Her husband had gained a few miles.

Then Creator caused a great forest to grow up in her way. The trees were so close together that she passed through this forest with great difficulty and it took several long hours to reach the end.

The trees did not stop her, but they slowed her down. Her husband gained several more hours.

Then Creator caused a great field of low-growing plants

to grow up around the woman as she rested. The plants were hung with bright red berries that sparkled in the sunlight.

She picked one and ate it.

"This is the most delicious berry I've ever eaten," the woman decided. "I'll fill my basket and take these berries home to my mother."

So she dumped all her possessions out of her basket and began picking the tiny berries.

As she picked the berries she ate some, too. Then it was that she began to think, "I miss my husband. I love him as much as I ever did. I should forgive him."

It took a very long time to fill her basket with such tiny berries. So when the man came over the hill and saw her sitting among the berries, he ran to her and fell down begging her forgiveness.

Naturally she had some doubt concerning his sincerity, but he promised repeatedly that he would never speak to her in an unkind manner again and would always treat her with love and respect.

At last she said, "Yes, I forgive you."

Then the man looked at her red stained fingers. "You're hurt," he cried, pressing his lips into the palms of her hands.

"No, no," she said, "it's the juice from these wonderful little berries."

Then she put one in his mouth.

He put one in her mouth.

She put another one in his mouth... and so it went for quite some time.

Then the woman got up and went home with her husband.

She called the little fruit heart berries because they stopped her in the field and changed her heart toward her husband.

So they were together for many years and when he went to the other side, she was lonely again.

But she picked berries with her grandchildren every summer and as they sat in the fields picking heart berries, she told them about the long ago time.

"These are the berries that made us sweethearts again," she would say, and it made the children glad.

Today the bright little red fruits are called strawberries, but it still gladdens the children to hear the story of how Creator brought them forth.

CHIPMUNK GETS HIS STRIPES

One day Wanabozho was walking through the forest, talking to his animal friends and admiring the trees, shrubs and other plants.

Suddenly he heard a great chattering and looking about he saw Chipmunk running back and forth beneath a tall pine tree.

Then he looked up into the high branches and saw his Uncle Owl trying to sleep. So he sat down to see what would happen.

When Owl closed his eyes, Chipmunk would begin his little chucking song. Then Owl would open an eye and look down and Chipmunk would be quiet. So Owl would close his eyes and Chipmunk would start in again.

"Oh," thought Wanabozho, "what a silly little pest. Doesn't he know Uncle Owl could finish him off with one good squeeze?"

Owl knew that, too. He also knew that he could not get any sleep as long as Chipmunk went on teasing him.

So he asked Chipmunk to go away.

"I need my rest," Owl said politely. "I've been out hunting all night and carrying urgent messages to the people. Please, go away, be quiet and let me sleep."

But Chipmunk would not go away. Nor would he be quiet. He was having too much fun teasing the old Owl.

Now Wanabozho could see that, although Owl remained calm and composed, he was losing patience with the little pest.

Then, when he could stand it no longer, Owl leaped from the tree and swooped down at Chipmunk with his great talons spread.

The naughty little Chipmunk knew he'd gone too far and quickly ran toward a hole in a nearby tree.

But Owl's outstretched claws grazed Chipmunk's back just as he dived into the safety of the dark hole.

Wanabozho said, "I saw what happened, little teaser. Now you will carry those marks for the rest of your life and everyone will know that you are a pest. Your children will be marked, too."

To this day it has remained so.

A BROKEN FRIENDSHIP

Cat and Mouse were once the best of friends. They were such excellent companions that Cat suggested, "We should live together. We can live quite comfortably in my big house, and we can use your small house to store our food."

So Mouse moved into Cat's house and they spent the summer and fall gathering food and getting to know each other better.

Cold-maker came with snow and wind, and winter fell upon the forest. But they had no worry for they had plenty of food stored at Mouse's house.

Then it happened that Mouse was invited to a naming ceremony.

"One of my relatives has had a child," Mouse told Cat. "They want me to come and give the child a name. It's an honor that I cannot refuse."

So he went away. He was gone for three days.

When he returned, Cat asked, "Did you have a good time?"

"Oh, my! I certainly did!"

"What did you do?"

"Oh, we sang and danced. We ate and drank. We told stories and I named that baby, too."

"What did you name the baby?"

"Ata Little Bit."

"Oh," said Cat, "that's a really cute name for a little one."

Then it happen that Mouse was invited to another naming ceremony.

Cat said, "I get kind of lonely around here. I never get to go to naming ceremonies. Do you think I could go along with you this time?"

"Oh, no!" Mouse said, "Some of my friends and relatives are afraid of you."

Cat was shocked, "But I do no harm!"

"Well, you're awfully big and you frighten the little ones."

"Tell them that I am kind and gentle."

"Yes," Mouse promised, "I'll do that."

Then he left.

After three day he returned looking plump and happy.

"Did you have a good time?" Cat asked.

"Yes! We danced, sang, ate, drank, told stories and I named the baby."

"What did you name the baby this time?"

"Ata Little More."

Cat thought friend Mouse didn't have much imagination because he'd named both babies Ata. But he didn't say anything as he didn't want to hurt his little friend's feelings.

Then Mouse was invited to another naming ceremony.

"Did you ask if I can come, too?" Cat wanted to know.

"Yes, I did. But no one wanted you to come. They all feel that you're just too dangerous and that you might hurt someone."

"But did you tell them that I am kind and gentle?"

"Of course, but they didn't believe me."

So mouse left.

Now Cat began to suspect that his little friend was up to something.

So when Mouse returned and Cat noticed that he was plumper than ever, he asked, "What did you name the baby this time?"

Mouse fell down laughing. "This time I named the baby Ate It All."

Now Cat knew that Mouse had eaten their entire food supply.

"That was a terrible thing for you to do!" Cat said. "That was food we gathered together. That was food we were going to share.

"You're selfish, greedy and dishonest! I don't want to be your friend anymore."

Then Cat picked up Mouse and threw him far out into the snow.

To this day, Cat and Mouse are not friends, and whenever Cat finds a mouse, he eats it because he still remembers how mouse lied, and cheated him out of his fair share of their winter food supply.

WANABOZHO BRINGS THE FIRE

There was a time in the long, long ago when the Anishinabeg had no fire to keep them warm or cook their food.

In fact, they feared fire because they had seen what it could do to the forest when lightening struck.

But when Wanabozho saw the effect of the cold on his kind grandmother, Nookomis, he decided she needed fire to warm her old bones. He told her he was going to steal some fire for her so she wouldn't be cold anymore.

Now fire was kept in the underworld by an old warrior magician who lived there with his two strong daughters. The magician guarded and protected the fire. The people had been told that the magician was powerful and quite vicious.

So Nookomis was frightened for her grandson.

"No!" she said. "That old magician will hurt you."

But Wanabozho was very brave and also quite determined. Once he made up his mind to do something... he did it.

So in the moon of wild rice, he started out for the place where fire was kept. When he got close, he hid his canoe in the trees by the river.

Then he changed into a little rabbit and jumped into the water to get wet. He wanted to look pitiful so the old man's daughters would feel sorry for him.

The women were hanging their fishing nets when one of them saw the wet rabbit. Feeling sorry for the little creature, she picked him up and carried him inside where her father was sleeping. She placed him near the fire to dry and get warm. Then she went back to help her sister with their work.

Wanabozho hopped closer to the fire and his steps woke up the old man. But when he saw that it was just an innocent rabbit, he went back to sleep.

When the old magician started snoring, Wanabozho changed himself into a man, grabbed a stick of fire and ran from the lodge

The magician woke up with an angry scream.

"Bring back my fire!" he roared.

Then he sent his daughters after Wanabozho, who was running as fast as he could toward the river.

But, looking back, he saw that the women were gaining on him.

"Give our fire back to us!" they called.

Just as Wanabozho reached the canoe he looked back again and saw a large meadow of dried grass.

"Here's your fire!" he cried as he plunged the burning stick into the dry grass. Instantly the grass was in a blaze and the wind carried the flames and smoke back toward the women. So they were forced to give up the chase.

Wanabozho pushed his canoe down into the water and began paddling toward his village. He was thinking about Nookomis and how warm she would be now.

As he looked back to watch the fire, he noticed how it was reflected in the leaves of the trees. He saw how they shone with brilliant colors of red, yellow, gold and brown.

It was so beautiful that he asked Creator to make the leaves look that way every fall...and so they have.

When he returned to his village with the gift of fire, he found that Nookomis had dug a shallow pit in the floor of their wigwam. She'd already lined the pit with round stones from the river, laid a bed of torn birchbark and built a little tipi of dry sticks. She had more wood waiting nearby.

She was sitting alone in the wigwam when Wanabozho came.

He touched the stick of fire to the birchbark and they watched it ignite. Then he waited for the sticks to burn. Afterwards he laid the heavier wood in the fire and sat down with his grandmother.

Although she was pleased that her grandson had done this thing, she told him,

"You took a terrible risk."

Wanabozho thought for a moment. Then he said, "I don't believe the magician has any real power, or he would have used it against me."

Then after a few minutes of further consideration, Nookomis replied, "It's quite possible that Creator allowed you to overcome the magician's power so an old woman could sit by the fire and warm her bones."

Perhaps they were both right.

LONG LEGS

n the far back times, all the birds of Turtle Island looked alike.

They were all one big tribe and all spoke the same language. They even built their lodges alike and lived together in a huge village among the tall trees where they ate the same kind of food.

Creator saw that this was not good and decided to make some changes.

Now this village was near a shallow stream and the birds enjoyed bathing and drinking in the clear waters. They liked to eat the weed seeds and tiny berries that grew there.

But sometimes they would peek over the bank, look at themselves in the clear water and wonder why they all looked alike.

One day Creator told them that the small shallow stream was going to flood and spread out over a wide bed.

"The slow shallow stream will soon become a great rushing river," Creator said. "You must move to the high meadow where you will be safe. There I have prepared a shallow pond for you."

Some of the birds were quick to follow Creator's instructions.

But others didn't like this idea. They thought they were wise enough to look after themselves and didn't want to be told what to do. So they refused to move.

Then the flood came. Suddenly the disobedient birds were caught in the midst of it. They were tossed about like bits of foam. Their wings were heavy with water and their short legs could not reach the bottom.

"We are drowning!" they screamed.

Some of the birds who lived in the meadow began to pray for them.

"Creator, it's true that these bird were very foolish children. But now they are really quite sorry they disobeyed you. Will you please make our legs longer so we can wade out into the river and rescue them?"

Creator was pleased and smiled on the water. The river became calm. Then a gentle breeze moved over the water to float the naughty birds toward the edge of the river where the water was more shallow.

Then Creator spoke to the birds that had prayed. "Look at yourselves. Now you have stilts with which to wade into deeper water than you've ever been in before. So go now, and rescue my disobedient children."

The birds looked down and saw that this was true. They even had long beaks!

So they waded into the water and began to trill in a loud chorus to let the frightened birds know they were coming to rescue them.

Since that day, wading birds still have long legs and beaks. All bird clans have different colored feathers and sing different songs, as well. They build different kinds of homes in a variety of places, and eat insects as well as seeds and fruit.

The long-legged birds are known as cranes and we honor them as birds of wisdom and courage.

They say that crane clans help us to become good speakers and storytellers. These helpers give us the courage needed to stand before large groups of people and speak the words that must be spoken.

THE MAGIC MOCCASINS

Some people say that it was Wanabozho who proved that the earth was round. They say he traveled to many places in his magic moccasins. But he never made war on the people he met, nor did he try to take their lands.

It was very, very long ago when he first thought that he would like to meet people of other cultures and nations. He wanted to find out more about them. So he put on the magic moccasins, then journeyed around the world and back.

It happened in this way.

He told his people that the earth was round. They pretended to be surprised, but he didn't know they were pretending.

Because roundness is the shape of life, they already knew the earth was round. But they wanted to play a trick on him. So they said, "A-wah! You lie!"

Now Wanabozho was a proud man and could not allow them to insult him with this manner of doubt. Therefore, he decided to prove that what he said was true.

"I will start from here today," he told them. "I will go west. I will keep going in a straight line toward the sunset. One day you will see me coming back from the east."

So he put on his magic moccasins and went on his way.

After some time he came to a small, ice-covered lake.

He ran toward it and tried to slide across on the ice. But the lake was not covered with ice. It was so calm and smooth that it looked frozen...but it was not.

No one saw him, so he laughed at himself and built a little fire to dry himself. Then he went to sleep. In the morning, he put on his magic moccasins and walked across the lake on top of the water.

When he came to a range of mountains, his magic moccasins allowed him to climb over them with ease.

Beyond the mountains was a vast ocean. The moccasins carried him safely over the salt water. It was a long crossing and he saw many strange things. There were whales and sharks, dolphins and octopi.

Sometimes, as he sat on the ocean to rest, small curious fish would appear under him. They'd gather around and stare up at the strange being traveling over their world. When he stuck his hands down into the water, they nibbled at his fingers and hurried away in alarm.

Wanabozho even walked through several violent ocean storms. Oh, how the water rose and fell. Sometimes he stood on a high mountain of water, other times he found himself in a valley. Eventually he was back on land again.

He went on walking without giving a thought to the seasons or the weather or the passing of time. He met many people and stayed with some of them for several moons.

They exchanged stories, songs, and dances. When they held their children and talked about their ancestors, Wanabozho yearned for home.

In most places he was received with courtesy and respect. But there was a nation of bearded men that tried to enslave him. With his magic moccasins, it was a simple matter to escape from them.

Once more he crossed the ocean. He rode part of the way on an iceberg.

After many years of being far from home, he began to see familiar landscapes and realized that he would soon be among his own people again.

When he saw a calm lake that appeared to be covered with ice, he decided to go for a swim. So he took off his clothes and ran toward the water. When he reached the edge of the water, he dived in...but the water was covered with ice. So he fell on the hard ice, bumping his head and skinning his nose.

No one was watching, so he laughed at himself, put on his clothes and continued walking west.

When he returned among his people, they looked at him in a strange manner. But when he told them who he was, they welcomed him with a great feast.

He'd been gone so long that he was nearly forgotten. The generations that had seen him leave had been gone for a long time. None of them remained alive.

Wanabozho felt sorry that he had missed seeing his old friends before they went to the other side and vowed he would never take such a prolonged trip again.

CORN SPIRIT

Once, a certain people planted some ordinary corn and found themselves with an extraordinary harvest. On just a few small fields they had grown and gathered an amazing amount of good corn.

But instead of being grateful for their outstanding harvest, they had no respect for the Spirit of Corn. They became careless and wasteful.

They ate more than they needed; they didn't care for it properly; it got wet and rotted; they fed it to the dogs; and the children put it in small leather bags and played games with it.

When they had eaten all they could, they buried the rest near their summer village, to save for their winter needs.

Then they moved to their winter camp and the young warriors went hunting. But although they found that game was plentiful, they had no success in bringing any home. Even their best hunters seemed to be blind. The animals became more cunning and more fleet. Soon hunger and need came among these people.

So the elders decided it was time to eat the corn they had buried.

They sent a few warriors back to get the corn and told them to return in time to save them all from starvation.

But when the men reached the summer place, they found the stored corn had been carried away by mice and squirrels.

This terrible news was received with sorrow at the winter camp and the people tried in every way to discover the reason for their misfortune. They tried to understand why they should be so tormented.

They performed every ritual and ceremony they could remember. They sang ancient sacred songs and prayed far into the night.

Then it happened that one of the men who had taken part in the waste of corn was walking alone in the forest, sorrowing over the dreadful situation.

Suddenly he entered a large clearing. In the center of the clearing, high upon a mound stood a birch bark lodge.

When he approached the lodge, he heard pitiful moans coming from inside.

When he entered he saw a sickly, miserable looking old man stretched out naked on worn, dirty mats.

"See what a pitiful condition I have been reduced to by the people I loved?" the poor man cried. "I wanted to feed them and their children but they threw me away. They dragged me through the dirt. They let their dogs tear me. They let me rot. They did all these terrible things.

"But, my son, I am glad that you have seen how poorly I live. See, I have no water in my jug. No clothing and not even a leaf to cover me from the cold.

"Look, weeds have overrun my gardens and fierce animals prowl around at night. Soon I will be gone.

"Go and tell your people what has happened to their old friend... Corn Spirit."

The man was moved with compassion and promised to do this. But first he covered the old man with his own robe and filled his water jug.

Then he hurried back to his people and told them how he'd found the good Corn Spirit suffering alone in an awful state of poverty.

"It was our wastefulness that caused this," he told them. "In fact, it was the cause of all our own misfortune as well."

The people listened in amazement.

Then they made an offering to Corn Spirit and their hunters' luck returned.

So they managed to get through the remainder of the winter and eventually returned to their summer village.

There they found a small amount of seed corn that had been returned by the mice and squirrels who left it in baskets near the door of every lodge.

Quickly the people prepared their gardens and planted the corn.

Although they enjoyed another abundant yield that fall, they used the corn with great respect and as they prospered, so did Corn Spirit who had remained their friend throughout the ordeal.

EAGLE PROPHECY

One day, a strong young man was climbing a steep and stony hill. He'd been walking for hours and was quite tired. So he lay down to rest on a warm, rose-colored boulder.

As he looked up, he saw five eagles sitting in the trees around him. After several minutes of enjoying their beauty, he noticed that they were all looking upward. Turning his gaze to the same direction, he was surprised to see a large white eagle sitting in the top of the tallest pine tree.

As he watched, the five dark eagles began to change form and soon became Ojibwe men, while the white eagle was transformed into a pure white man with white hair and white eyes. From time to time, the white man stuck out his forked tongue to lick the sky and speak to the Ojibwe men.

Such a vision frightened the young man, but he continued to watch and was surprised to see the men turn back into birds.

Suddenly the white eagle spread his wings and flew down over the dark ones and with a great whistle compelled them to fly after him.

The young man sat for a long time considering the meaning of such a vision. Then he returned to his village and told the elders what he had seen.

All the elders appeared shaken.

"Yes," one said. "I have heard of such things. Other people are seeing visions of this nature. What you saw will some day come true. It means the day is coming when a race of white people will overcome us and we will be forced to follow their ways."

Another one said, "I don't know when they will come. Perhaps in your lifetime. I hope I never see them for their ways are not ours and their ways will bring us into great harm."

They went on to tell the young man other things he would need to know to make a good journey through life.

"You have a gift," an elder woman said. "Your eyes see into the future. Use the gift wisely and for the good of your people. Perhaps your gift of foresight will help the people prepare for the newcomers who will arrive with persuasive powers."

Then, one by one, the elders passed over and it wasn't long before the first white men arrived in the region. By then the young man had grown old, too.

Although the prophecy was remembered and had been spoken of often, when the newcomers came, no one could prevent them from taking what they wanted.

Then, as the eagle had prophesied, the Ojibwe became more and more like the white people and followed them into their harmful ways.

FROG VENGEANCE

An elder man had two sons, and each son had a son. The elder was proud of his sons and he loved his grandsons very much.

One day the three men were going out to hunt and the boys wanted to go, too. The men were pleased to see their children taking such an interest in providing food for the family, so they allowed the boys to accompany the hunting party.

The party went some distance from the village and made camp. Then they went out to see what they could find. But the boys grumbled and complained. They said they had already walked so far that they were too tired to hunt. Their loud whining frightened the game away.

So after a short time, the fathers took the boys back to camp. The elder returned later with a few partridges which he cleaned and cooked.

Once again, the boys complained. They said they didn't like partridge meat. They said it was too dry.

But Grandfather told them, "We must learn to be thankful for what we have and express gratitude to Creator for feeding us again."

Then they sat around the fire while Grandfather told a story of how the frog people took vengeance against those who were unkind to small, helpless creatures. Then one by one they rolled up in their blankets and went to sleep.

In the morning it was decided that the men would go hunting and the boys would remain in camp. Their fathers wanted them to rest and play.

"But you must keep the fire going," Grandfather said. "That will be your responsibility."

So the men left and the boys began gathering wood. Soon they had a large pile. While looking for more wood, they discovered that there were many frogs in the area. So they caught a few.

They carried them to camp, tossed them into the fire and watched their desperate struggle to escape the painful flames. The boys found this an amusing way to pass the day. So by the time the men returned, many frogs had been killed.

When Grandfather saw what had happened, he was appalled.

"You have done a terrible thing!" he cried. "You killed these small creatures for no other reason than that you found pleasure in their misery and death. These helpless creatures died in torment and terror. You had no pity for them! Neither shall you find pity when torment and terror falls upon you."

"Come, come," one of the men said. "Don't let yourself be so upset over a few dead frogs."

The other one said, "You're being unreasonable toward these boys. Don't forget... they are still children."

So they excused their sons for what they had done to the frog people.

But Grandfather insisted, "A terrible act has been committed against these defenseless ones and a terrible thing will be done to you."

The men were disgusted with the old man.

One of them said, "I've lost interest in hunting."

"Yes," said the other. "I think we should go home."

So Grandfather, his sons and grandsons broke camp and began walking toward the village.

But on their way, they came to a great bog which none of them remembered crossing before.

One of the men said, "We will walk across here."

But Grandfather was troubled by the unusual way the bog had suddenly appeared. "It's not safe to cross this strange bog," he told them. "We should go around."

"No," the boys whined. "We're too tired to go around! We want to cross here!"

Grandfather did not want to argue with them, so he said, "You may do what seems best to you. I will go around."

So he left them there.

When he got to the village he was surprised to find that they had not yet arrived.

Immediately he went back to find them, but they had completely disappeared and they were never seen again.

To the end of his days, the elder told the story of the frogs' vengeance.

"It is wrong to torment small, helpless creatures, " he would say. "Furthermore, fathers make a great mistake when they fail to correct the conduct of their children."

TOO MANY RULES

Long ago, a certain nation grew resentful toward Creator because they thought the great code of life had been unfairly imposed upon them.

Creator's code consisted of two laws: never take more than you need and respect your relatives.

Now these people knew that failure to live by these laws would be harmful to all other nations. They also knew that Creator would not be pleased if any part of Turtle Island suffered because the code of life had been violated. So they tried to hide their behavior from Creator.

But Coyote sat on his high hill where he was able to see everything these people did and he wondered at the deceptive conduct of the pathetic nation.

"How can they be so ignorant?" he thought. "How can they believe that Creator does not see what they are doing?"

Coyote found these people quite entertaining. He laughed at them, because they were always glancing sideways over their shoulders to see if they were being watched.

One day Coyote went to speak to these strange people. He sat at the edge of their village and waited for someone to acknowledge him. The few people who saw him sitting there turned away quickly because they thought if they ignored him, he'd leave.

At last a small child, too young for fear, came right up to Coyote. "Who are you?" asked the little one.

"I am your friend," said Coyote in a gentle voice.

Several other children approached him and soon the adults began to come near.

"Greetings, my friends," Coyote called. "Have no fear."

One of the men asked timidly, "Are you a spy? Were you sent by Creator to report our conduct?"

"Oh, no," Coyote chuckled. "I'm far too ordinary for such important work."

Then Coyote complained loudly about Creator's great code of life and how difficult it had made all his days.

Naturally the people agreed with Coyote and began to explain why they had grown suspicious, nervous and full of fear.

"We have decided not to live by Creator's code of life," one of the women declared.

"But we are afraid we will be discovered doing something that violates those laws," someone else said.

Coyote closed his eyes and appeared to listen respectfully. From time to time he nodded his head slowly in a solemn manner.

But he was really quite delighted because he knew that these fearful people were also fools. So, he decided to have some fun at their expense and he opened his bag of tricks.

Coyote sat tall on his hindquarters and puffed himself up with importance. Then he cleared his throat several times and the people waited quietly for him to speak.

"I know how you can rid yourselves of your fear of Creator," he announced at last.

"How? How?' the excited people cried in unison.

"Elect the people you want to govern you, and create your own code of life. Then appoint others to enforce the new rules. Reward those who follow the rules and punish those who do not."

Then Coyote yawned, shook his bushy tail and trotted off to his hill to see what would happen to this foolish nation.

"What a wonderful idea!" said the man who most frequently violated Creator's great code of life. His guilty fear had destroyed any love or respect he ever had for creation.

This man saw an opportunity to be important. He wanted to make laws and assign punishment. The rest of the people wanted to feel important too. The more important they felt, the less important Creator seemed to be.

Immediately they nominated and elected several people to govern and begin the task of making rules. The elected officials were instructed to make lots of rules because the more rules the people had, the safer they felt.

Of course, they stopped following Creator's good laws.

In fact, they pretended that those laws no longer existed.

But, oh, how they loved their own rules.

There were rules designating who could walk which paths through the forest. There were rules concerning who, when, where and what certain people could hunt. There were rules about when and where one could gather wood. There were even rules concerning when and how one should honor Creator!

Soon the rule-makers began collecting fees and issuing permits which entitled the permittee to use certain paths a specific number of times before renewing the permit. Hunting and gathering rights also had to be paid for.

Coyote laughed at the foolish people and their arrogant leaders. He laughed because now they were paying each other for the things Creator had freely given to be used by all for the welfare of all.

Those who governed became powerful and wealthy and overworked, so they appointed officials to establish a tax code and others to collect the taxes.

The government grew even more cumbersome and created new laws daily. Soon more officials were needed to enforce the abundance of laws, creating a law enforcement industry.

Those who could not pay were confined and guarded. This created yet another industry which added to the tax burden.

They had created a hungry government, a government that ate up resources, destroyed communities, and robbed people of their dignity.

Today the deluded nation continues to serve their debauched government. Many still believe the illusion that their laws make them superior and keep them safe.

Those few individuals who know they are living an illusion try to face Creator with honor. But they are penalized for their respectful conduct because it does not reflect favorably on the man-made establishment.

Coyote is still watching and laughing at the great joke he played on the foolish nation. For the pathetic people are in bondage to a lesser code and have burdened themselves with many unnecessary laws, when Creator gave but two.

WANABOZHO RETURNS

One day the elected tribal officials were having a meeting at the tribal headquarters in Cass Lake. They had met to talk about reservation problems and seek solutions. But because of deficient funds and a per diem squabble, they were making no progress.

So, one of the elected men went for a walk along the lake. While he was walking... he was thinking. Then a strange thing happened. He met Wanabozho.

At first he couldn't believe what he saw. But Wanabozho stood before the man and said, "My son, you look troubled."

The man said, "Yes, I am troubled. The people have lost confidence in the Reservation Business Committee and the Executive Counsel of the Minnesota Chippewa Tribe. Yet we really are trying to determine what will be best for all the people. There are only a few good jobs. So many of our people do not live well. Fathers are discouraged. Many leave their families. Mothers are discouraged. Some will not care for their children. Many children are quite unhappy. It is a poor time for budget cuts."

"Yes," Wanabozho replied. "I have seen the human pain in this community. I too am troubled by so much sorrow. I am also puzzled, for I remember when there was enough good work for everyone to do. The people lived well. Fathers were proud to provide for their families. Mothers were pleased to care for their children. The children honored their parents and were happy."

"Ah," the elected man sighed. "We hope to restore such domestic tranquility. We have established numerous programs to overcome the despair that is rampant on this reservation."

Wanabozho went on speaking. "There were many deer. Enough for all. Enough to share. The sinew made strong thread. The hides were rubbed with brains to make them soft. They were smoked over a slow fire. They made fine garments. It was good and pleasant work. The meat was cut, sliced thin and chopped fine. It was mixed with herbs and vegetables to make good meals. Nothing was wasted, nothing was scorned."

The elected man explained that the reservation had a food distribution program and Social Services could provide clothing vouchers. He assured Wanabozho that the people would have what they needed.

But Wanabozho did not seem to be listening.

He took something from his pocket. He showed the man that he had one dollar in coins. He laid the money on a rock and continued to speak. "Long ago the people lived as they would. They lived with the land and they lived with the times. Now we see that many things have changed. Brother deer is bought and sold. Our children become merchandise when elected Indian officals collect state and federal funds that never reach those who need it most."

The elected man raised his voice. "You will find that compromise is often essential."

"Even in this time, with confusion everywhere, I understand this much," Wanabozho continued. "The people cannot return to our old ways and you cannot lead as our fathers led. Tell the people they must make a place for themselves in this new time."

The man was encouraged. He felt that he had found some answers. He was excited and eager to return to the meeting.

He put out his hand toward Wanabozho, but Wanabozho stepped back and turned his face away.

Wanabozho spoke once more, "Tell me, my son, why have you continued to overlook the exploitation of my children? Why do you reward courtesy with contempt? Why do you honor greed? How do you justify the oppression of your brothers? How do you explain the institution of nepotism in a way that those excluded from benefits can appreciate? How can I get government money and casino profits for myself?"

Suddenly the man was alone. He thought, "Perhaps I have been dreaming."

But when he turned to leave, he saw the coins shining in the sun.

When he returned to the meeting he said nothing, for he was ashamed.

THE WOMAN WHO MADE DRUMS

It happened early one morning in the long ago that a certain village which stood near Father Waters in the midst of Turtle Island was invaded by men who came from the east.

The dawn attack was swift and terrible. The old people of the village tried to hide in their lodges, those with strength ran into the woods, young mothers fell down with their arms around their children. No one expected mercy... none was given.

But one young woman had run into the river and stood among the rushes, breathing through a hollow reed. There she remained all day and into the long night.

As she stood in the cold, black water, she considered what terrible things had happened to her people. At last she was overwhelmed by grief and despair. So she decided that she would go with them to the other side.

Suddenly she heard someone speaking to her. The voice told her that she would not be killed. She would live! She would go forth and remind all peoples of the original instructions.

The people would rediscover how they could live in peace, harmony and balance. They would find within themselves all they needed to live well and prosper. Nations would no longer find it necessary to fight other nations for territory, resources and status.

"But war is inevitable," the woman reasoned. "It has always been so, and always so shall be."

"No," the voice returned sadly, "it has not. But many things have been forgotten. Nevertheless, I will show you a better way. I will teach you the way of peace."

Then it was that the woman received a vision of twelve drums. She'd seen drums before, small personal hand drums like the men in her village carried about with them. But these new drums were so large that several men could gather around them. These drums had great voices, too.

In the vision she saw herself going across the land to live among the peoples of many nations. She watched herself gather materials for the construction of the drums she dreamed. One by one she made them. The people listened to her words and, as work on the drum progressed, they learned the way of peace.

"Now you must leave the water," the voice told her.

"I will certainly be killed," the woman thought.

"No one will see you," the voice promised. "You will walk in the midst of these powerful invaders and you will not be harmed. You will live to make the drums you saw in your vision."

So the woman rose up from the water, walked through the village and went out into the nations. The enemy did not see her pass among them.

She lived a long and prayerful life dedicated to the creation of sacred drums.

In the end she made twelve. Then she was called to the other side. So twelve great nations were reminded of the original instructions and learned to live in peace, harmony and balance.

Then it happened that Turtle Island was invaded by powerful men from far away who were carried over the great salt waters by large swimming birds.

These men had no knowledge of the original instructions and no respect for the message of peace, harmony and balance.

After many years there was no place on Turtle Island where their feet had not touched. Everywhere they went, they carried greed, corruption, violence and death.

Of course, the woman had warned the twelve nations that such peoples would arrive. She'd told them the newcomers would bring vile spirits. These spirits would live in the fire water the invaders carried.

"You must not drink this," she'd repeated again and again.

But after several generations, her words were forgotten and many peoples of the first nations of Turtle Island were enslaved by the vile spirits that lived in the fire water.

Then it happened that the drums began to disappear.

One day they were in the midst of the people... the next day they were gone!

But in that place where the woman had made the first drum, an elder man remembered her words of warning. He'd heard them from his father, who'd heard them from his mother, who had heard them from her father.

He had been told, "When these vile spirits come to this nation, you must protect the drum. You will do this by remembering the songs of this drum. You will carry the drum out to the arbor every morning. You will sing and pray. On a certain night you will dream. Then Creator will give you a vision of what must be done to protect the drum... and you will do it."

So it happened one day that the drum was silent. The people who lived in that village awakened under a dark sky and found that the sacred drum was gone!

But this ancient drum had not disappeared. The elder man had hidden it. Where? No one knows. For when he passed over, he took the secret with him. He could not disclose its location to anyone, for many had been defiled by the spirits that lived in the fire water that the invaders had brought to the village.

But somewhere in the heart of Turtle Island, an infant has been born. This little one is growing in strength and knowledge. Here is a child of wisdom and courage. Here is a child that will dream a dream. This child will remember the original instructions.

Perhaps this one will find the last sacred drum. Perhaps this one will create a new one. But what will surely be done is this! The child will mature and go out to teach other nations.

Many will listen, some will hear, and a few will choose the way of peace, harmony and balance. Others will continue to endure the captivity brought to first nation peoples by the newcomers who arrived long ago on the wings of great floating birds.

It might happen that the teacher will be persecuted for failing to conform to the lesser expectations of a people who have lost their original instructions and have no respect for messengers of peace, harmony and balance.

It might happen that the teacher will be accepted and the people will treasure the original instructions. They will learn to walk in peace, harmony and balance, and the song of sacred drums will once again welcome the dawn.

UNGRATEFUL PEOPLE

When man was put into creation he came with a lot to learn.

So he watched the birds and animals. They taught him about food and medicine. They showed him how to survive. Creator also gave man spirit helpers to make his journey easier. These helpers are still watching over the people today.

Man learned that all things have spirit... even trees.

Eventually, people began living in groups so they could share resources and responsibilities.

Now it happened when the time of hunger was upon the land that a certain band of hunters and gatherers found game becoming scarce in their area. While they had been quite generous during the time of plenty, they found sharing difficult as they watched their food dwindle away.

So it happened one morning that a young warrior rose early and went out to greet the morning sun. He thanked Creator for protecting the people and giving them another day to live. Then he asked for immediate intervention.

"My brothers and sisters are suffering. The children are crying because they are hungry. The elders are grieving in deep sorrow as they watch hunger reduce us to selfish conduct.

"Please provide the nourishment we need until the

earth warms and food is once again available for all. The hungry time is passing, but we need help now."

As he stood praying, he heard a voice calling to him.

"Come here! I'm over here!"

The man saw nothing, but the voice went on calling.

Soon a flock of birds landed in a tree nearby and began pecking at the limbs and branches. The man walked closer and watched them. He noticed a spot on the tree where the bark was torn and a thick amber sap was seeping out.

He touched it and found it sticky. He licked his fingers and found it sweet. He ate more. Almost immediately he felt strength flowing into his body.

He said a joyful prayer of thanksgiving and called the people out to eat of this new food. In their excitement they tore the bark loose and had their fill.

In the weeks that followed, they went out and helped themselves to more of the nourishing sap whenever they were hungry. They no longer went out hunting because the new food was always available. Some of the people got so lazy that they just laid under a tree and let the sap run into their mouths.

They never stopped to offer thanks to the maple tree spirits.

Naturally, the maple tree spirits were displeased and

asked Creator to bring these ungrateful people into an awareness of the great gift they were now taking for granted.

So Creator caused it to start raining. Oh, it rained and rained and rained. When the people ran to the trees for syrup, they found the sap as thin as water. Only a hint of flavor remained.

Now they could not get enough nourishment from one tree, so they ran about tearing bark from many trees. But they were all the same. There was no more syrup.

Then they heard the voice of Creator. "For being ungrateful and wasteful, you will have to work hard to enjoy the strengthening food that was so freely given.

"Furthermore, it will not be available all year long. Only in the early spring will the sap flow.

"Therefore, you must collect, boil and prepare enough to see you through the whole year.

"The tree spirits will tell you what to do. But I want you to be thankful and grateful to the trees and other plant nations. Respect all things, live in harmony and prosper."

The maple tree spirits told the people how to tap the maple trees with a narrow slash in the bark.

The cedar tree spirits told them how to carve cedar spoons. These were to be put into the slash from which the sap would flow. The spoon would guide the sap into a catching dish.

The birch tree spirits told them how to make birch bark catching dishes to gather the sap that dripped from the cedar spoon.

Then the sap had to be boiled until it reached the stage of syrup. Further preparation gave the people maple sugar and maple sugar cakes.

Creator also said, "Maple syrup time will be a time of hard work. It will also become a community celebration of respect for other nations, and sharing with those who are unable to work in the sugar bush."

So it was that an ungrateful, wasteful, selfish people learned to be thankful again, to appreciate other nations and share the good gifts Creator provided for all.

FLYING BONES

One day two young boys told their father that they were going to paddle their canoe across the lake. They promised to return that evening with a wonderful gift for their kind mother.

They left with their father's consent and their mother's blessing.

Now these boys were not only brothers, but good friends and enjoyed being together. They were having such fun that they failed to notice a gathering of storm clouds in the north.

Suddenly a violent wind swept them far from land and

they were lost on the dark water.

The storm continued into the night and the parents were full of fear for the boys. The father was angry with himself for allowing them to go, and the mother was angry with herself for not trying to stop them.

The howling of the wind and the crashing of the waves against the black rocks made it difficult to hear. But someone was shrieking in terror. The mother and father thought their children were crying for them and they ran along the edge of the lake calling their names.

During a sudden lull, there came an answer to their cries but it was not the voice of either boy.

Then there came another shriek and a bolt of lightening lit the night. Looking up they saw a grotesque creature wedged in the high rocks, struggling to free itself.

When it saw the man and woman, the creature began to whine in a whistling voice, "Help me! Pity me! I beg you!"

The woman froze in horror.

But the man called out, "I dare not! A living being should not touch such a creature as you. For it is not natural for the dead to return asking help from those who are still live."

But the pitiful creature went on crying. "Help me! Have pity! I am not dead! I am Flying Bones. My destiny is ever to wail of my faults and spend forever in the skies. To be blown about by the winds. To be chilled by the cold and scorched by the sun."

At last the woman spoke, "Why must you live this way?"

So Flying Bones told his story:

I was once the only son of a mother and father who pampered me. I grew up to be cruel and selfish. Not only was I disrespectful to my parents and other elders, but abusive toward other children.

So my parents suffered because they raised me to expect too much for myself. Then their lives were full of grief and worry because of my bad ways. Other people complained about me, too.

My father was humiliated by those who denounced me. So he decided that I should be left in a tree to starve. He made a nest of twigs and sticks in the crutch of a tall tree where I was to stay until I died of hunger.

My mother kissed my hands and gave me a good blanket.

But my father shouted as they went away, "Ravens and buzzards, I leave you a young boy. He is no good, but you can have him."

Yes, these were his last words for me... his own son!

After I had cried for a long time, I decided to meet my end with courage. So I climbed up into the nest to wait for death.

On the fortieth day of hunger I was in an emaciated condition. My body was no more than skin and bones. That night I heard the voice of the spirit of blame.

"Little boy," the voice said, "now you have suffered enough. Your misdeeds were the result of those who allowed you to live in such an uncaring way. You were too young to know what you were doing and your father did not give you proper guidance. Instead of leaving you here, he should have taken you home and trained you to be a better person.

"Therefore, I will give you a knife and the power to fly. You will retain your emaciated condition but you will be strong. The knife will always be sharp and you can use it to open the bellies of certain people while they sleep. You will fly in the air and your bones will rattle as you travel. Your voice will be sharp and whistling. When certain people hear you coming, they will fall asleep. While they are unconscious you will open them with the knife and take the fat from their stomachs. Then you will spit into their bellies and close them up. When they awaken they will seem to be quite normal for awhile. But after three winters they will die.

"You can only travel during cold clear nights when your

voice can be heard from far away. But you will not prey on those who know your story and have sympathy for your situation."

Then with my sharp knife and a shrill cry I flew out of the nest and headed north. My skin was dark and clung to my bones like old leather, but I was so strong that I never stopped for rest.

So I traveled to a cold land and stayed there during the warm seasons. Then as I was returning in the fall I came upon one of the men who had denounced me. He was traveling with a party of six.

The man was sitting in the midst of his companions when he heard the rattle of my bones and the whistle of my cry. He fell on his side and went to sleep. His friends tried to wake him, but they could not.

When they saw me, they froze in terror and watched as I cut their sleeping companion. I took the fat from his stomach and spit into his belly. They watched as the wound healed and the man went on sleeping.

Then I flew away.

Three years later the man was dead from a wasting disease.

Since then I have cut many others. Some of them are still waiting to die.

That was the story Flying Bones told.

• • •

"But if you will set me free," he promised, "no harm will come to you."

The man was repulsed by Flying Bones, but he also felt sorry for him. So he began removing the rocks that held him.

Suddenly the creature was free.

Up he went! Whistling and wailing and rattling across the dark sky!

In the morning the storm had passed and the two boys returned to their parents.

They told them that they had found refuge on an island and waited for the storm to break up so they could get back home.

They said they had heard a strange wailing cry and the rattle of bones throughout their ordeal.

They said that in the flashes of lightening they saw a man in the canoe with them. He was no more than skin and bones, but he was very strong and paddled their canoe to a sheltered place on the island. He pulled the canoe up on the rocks and they leaped out to run away from him. But he caught them in his hard bony hands and pushed them under the overturned canoe. Quickly he piled several fallen branches over them and suddenly . . . he was gone.

"Poor Flying Bones!" their mother cried. "Poor, poor spirit."

Then she fell down and kissed her children's hands.

THE BIRTH OF WANABOZHO

When the world of the Anishinabeg was destroyed by the great flood, Creator took pity on the people and sent a teacher to help them make their way in the new world.

Now the birth of the teacher came about in this way:

A wise elder woman named Nookomis fell in love with a handsome stranger. Many of her friends tried to discourage her from marrying the man. They told her that such a relationship at her time in life would jeopardize her status among the people.

Nookomis decided to risk her place in the community, and the man took her to the moon where they arrived young and strong. They lived there for quite some time and they were happy together.

But a jealous woman decided that she wanted the man for herself and began planning how to get rid of his wife.

One day she saw Nookomis sitting alone on the edge of a crater lake. Quickly she ran up behind her and pushed her into the deep water.

So it was that Nookomis fell all the way back to earth. When she returned, she was just as old and gray as the day she went to the moon with her husband. Of course, she was lonely for awhile.

Then, to her delight, she discovered that she was pregnant!

Soon she gave birth to a daughter and named her Wenona. The gentle girl grew tall and kind. Many young men wanted her, but Nookomis would not give her to any of the braves.

Then it happened that the West Wind saw Wenona bathing in the lake with some other young women and he fell in love with her. When he went back to his wind kingdom in the mountains, he could not forget her.

So he returned one night and carried Wenona to the mountains where he kept her in his lodge with his sons North, South, and East Winds.

Wenona escaped the mountains and found her way back to her grieving mother. Nookomis was happy again!

Not long after her return, Wenona gave birth to twin boys. Totally exhausted from the difficult labor of twin births, the gentle young woman went to the other side, taking one of the infants with her.

Of course, Nookomis felt great sorrow at the loss of her daughter and grandson.

She named the living infant Wanabozho, wrapped him in soft grass and placed him under a large wooden bowl to protect him from danger or accident. She only took him out to feed and clean him. Then she wrapped him in fresh grass and put him back under the bowl.

One day she heard a rustling, and lifted the bowl to

find that the infant had changed himself into a small rabbit. He had eaten the grass that she'd wrapped him in and was looking for more.

She picked him up and held him close for the first time. She was sorry that she'd left him alone under the bowl while she grieved.

Suddenly the rabbit changed into a boy who wrapped his arms around her neck and kissed her on the cheek. Then they wept together for those that had departed.

Nookomis loved the boy greatly and the child rarely left her side.

As Nookomis continued to age, the boy grew tall and strong.

He began to wander from her side more and more. He went into the forest where he learned many things about the plants, insects, birds, and other beings who lived on Turtle Island.

Because Wanabozho was both human and spirit, he could change himself into many things, but most of the time he took the form of a young, strong, brave man.

But he also had a great sense of humor and often did things just to make the people laugh.

He was a great help to the Anishinabeg.

He showed them how to hunt and fish, where to find roots and plants for food and medicine.

He also taught the children how to get along with all their relatives. He did this through stories, songs and deeds.

So it was that he became the mythical hero of the woodland people.

So it is that we are still telling of his deeds today.

THE VILLAGE BRAT

Not so long ago, a woman who lived at Leech Lake lost her husband during an influenza epidemic. She came near to losing her only child as well. But the little one survived and became so precious to the young widow that she could not bear to see the child disappointed in any way.

So it was that little Nellie became so rude and so spoiled that many referred to her as 'the village brat'. Still... her mother loved her dearly, as mothers will.

When the widow took her daughter out to visit, the child never failed to behave as badly as possible.

She would say to some, "Have you no other quilt to cover your bed? That one is so old and shabby that a dog wouldn't want it."

To another she would say, "Aren't you just sick of those dusty old curtains? You could at least wash them once in awhile."

Many times she would spill things or break cups. She would even throw the dishes if she didn't like the food she was offered.

Her poor mother was ashamed of the child's conduct and stopped visiting her friends and neighbors. She stayed home more and more.

But not Nellie. She would stand near the road and watch people go by. She would stare at the elders and stick her tongue out at other children. She pointed her fingers at those who were poorly dressed and even laughed at the lame woman who limped along.

In her own home she stamped her feet and screamed and shouted over all the things that did not please her. She spilled her soup and smashed bread on the floor with her feet saying, "I don't want to eat this!"

She tore her clothes during fits of anger and spoiled many nice dresses by rolling through the mud. Her mother was kept busy sewing and mending and cleaning and ironing the girl's clothes.

Never once did Nellie say she was sorry.

Not once did she try to help her mother in any way.

Now the neighbors never invited Nellie or her mother to their homes anymore. But Nellie would sometimes arrive uninvited. So they hid behind the door and pretended no one was home.

Nellie was not so easily fooled. She knew what was going on. So she would chase their chickens out of the coop, throw stones at the cow, pull the cat's tail, twist the dog's ears, and give the pig a good kick.

When the neighbors came out to stop her, she would stick out her tongue, scream and run away.

One day as she tormented a poor dog, he bit her on the leg. Nellie screamed a scream that would have raised the dead. The people came running to see who was being killed.

When they saw what had happened, one of the men said, "We can't shoot a good dog for biting the village brat. Such a cruel child needs a good switching."

Another said, "I agree, it's time she got a whipping."

Nellie was angry and frightened, so she ran away.

She ran to the lake where a family was drying their rice on large cattail mats. She ran through the rice, kicking it in all directions and scattering it in the grass. The people were shocked and shouted at her. "Stop! Stop!"

But out popped her tongue and away she ran.

When she came to a place where a family was picking cranberries, she found several baskets of fruit under a big tree. So she dumped out the berries, trampled them under her feet and jumped on the baskets until they were ruined.

Then she found a neat bundle of lunch and a jug of tea. She drank as much of the tea as she wanted and spilled the rest of it. She ate their sandwiches, too. What was left, she trampled into the ground.

Then she decided to go home. But after going a short distance she became very tired, so she climbed up into a tree and went to sleep. She slept until it was nearly dark and was awakened by loud voices. Looking down she was surprised to see a group of tiny old men.

One of them said, "Look at what she has done in just

one day. She tormented the dog, scattered the rice, ruined good food, spoke many bad words and has worried her poor mother sick."

Another said, "She needs a lesson."

A third added, "We could teach her a lesson she'd never forget."

Nellie knew they were talking about her and this kind of a threat made her mad. So she jumped out of the tree and walked up to them saying, "Well here I am! Now just what do you suppose you can do about that?"

Nellie was not afraid of them because they were so small.

Silently the little men joined hands and made a circle around her. Then they sang a magic song and when it was over Nellie found that she could not move. She was frozen into her usual position, her tongue sticking out of her mouth and her face caught in an ugly smirk.

She actually felt quite ridiculous. It was the first time she'd ever felt uncomfortable about making faces and sticking out her tongue. So she had already learned a good lesson. But it would take more than one lesson to straighten her out.

The leader of the little people called for the homeliest of their nation to step forward and they circled him. As Nellie watched, they breathed on him and he began to change. First he grew quite tall, as tall as Nellie. Then in an instant he changed into her very image. He looked exactly like her!

They took her pretty clothes and dressed him. They covered Nellie with an old potato sack.

Then the impostor climbed up in the tree and went to sleep.

That is where the search party found look-alike-Nellie the next morning. They could not awaken the girl, so they carried her home to the poor widow who carefully nursed the child who could not move a finger or wink an eye.

But in the field that fateful night, the little people tormented Nellie. They knocked her down, twisted her ears, pulled her hair, hit her with sticks and kicked her in the butt to remind her of all the unkind things she had done to the poor animals in the village.

Finally the spell was broken and Nellie ran off screaming with the little men right behind her. Around and around they went until she stumbled and fell into a dark hole. Over and over she tumbled, deeper and deeper into the earth, until she rolled into a small chamber in the underground world of the little people.

The leader came toward her and the others followed. They pointed at Nellie, whispering and giggling behind their tiny hands. Nellie did not like that. She glared at them and told them to stop. But they laughed at her and stuck out their little blue tongues.

Suddenly Nellie realized that she was very hungry. "I want to eat!" she demanded.

"Follow me," said the leader.

Now Nellie found that she could not walk upright in this small world so she crawled along behind the little man until they came to a large cavern. She saw that the entire floor was littered with cakes, breads, biscuits, cookies, meat, vegetables, fruit and many other things. But all the food was old and spoiled and dirty.

"I will not eat your garbage," she screamed.

But the little man said, "This is your garbage, Nellie. This is all the food you have ruined and wasted since you were first able to feed yourself."

Somehow Nellie knew the little man would not lie. But she stared at the awful mess and grumbled, "I don't care. I won't eat it."

"Yes, you will," the man said. "For you will get nothing else to eat until this is all gone."

Then one by one the little people left.

The man was right. For Nellie became so hungry that she couldn't help herself. It took her many weeks, but one day the garbage was gone. She'd eaten all of it.

Then the little people returned with fresh fruit, soft

biscuits, sweet jams, cold milk and warm cakes. Now Nellie ate gladly, but she didn't even think of saying 'thank you'.

"Now may I go home?" she asked. "I don't like it here."

"No, there's more for you to do."

Then she was taken to another large room with heaps and piles of dirty, torn laundry from one end to the other. Nellie knew that these were her clothes and she knew what she must do. Silently she began to pick up the clothes and the little people left. When they returned many weeks later, they found everything in order.

Every sock was clean, and darned. Every dress had been washed, carefully pressed and hung in a row along the wall. The underwear was carefully folded in neat stacks. Nellie looked around at what she'd done and was quite pleased with all she had accomplished.

When the little people returned, they agreed that she had done a good job.

"But now you must see your garden. This is the garden you have been planting since you were first able to speak. It is a garden grown with words. Every good, kind word has grown into a beautiful flower, an herb, or a useful food. All the bad, cruel words have grown into thistles and brambles and thorns."

So she crawled along behind the little man and they went to the garden.

When Nellie saw it she began to weep. Yes, her garden was nearly all weeds with very few little flowers struggling to grow among them.

Nellie turned to the little man and shouted a nasty word. She watched her word fall to the ground and grow up into a twisted stinging weed. Quickly she slapped a hand over her mouth and without another word, fell to her knees and began the most difficult lesson of all.

Silently she crawled slowly forward, pulling the thorns and thistles. In a very short time her hands were torn and bleeding. Her knees burned with pain and her back ached. Seeing this, the little people pitied her. So they knelt down and helped her until the job was done.

Now the garden spread before them cleared of weeds and ready to grow anything that Nellie would plant in it. She looked at the little people with their bleeding hands and scraped knees.

"Thank you," she said.

Then she saw the words fall into the garden and watched as a lovely little pink flower came springing up out of the earth.

"Now you may rest," the little man said. "It's time for you to go home."

Nellie awakened quite suddenly and found herself in her own bed, in her own home. As she sat looking about, the door opened and her mother entered, carrying a pail of water.

"Mother!" Nellie cried, jumped out of bed and ran to her.

The woman stared in amazement as Nellie took the heavy pail and set it on the table. Then they held each other for a long, long time. They cried together, for they were very happy.

"You've been sick for such a long time," Nellie's mother told her. "For two years you have not been able to move a finger or wink an eye."

So Nellie knew that she'd been with the little people for two years, as they worked to change her life into something good.

From that day forward she ate anything that was put in front of her and she was glad for it. She was no longer careless with her clothes and helped her mother in any way that she could. It is said that the neighbors grew to love her for her kindness.

Later she married and had children of her own. Now everyone will tell you that Nellie has the most respectful children that ever lived at Leech Lake.

COYOTE AND THE FRY BREAD

Coyote always played tricks on others, so now and then someone would trick him. Usually it happened when he was hungry and he let his stomach rule his brain.

One day he saw Fox, who was sitting on a little hill sunning himself and gazing off into the distance at a small pool of water.

Coyote asked, "What are you doing? You can't be sitting here like a fool right in plain sight? Someone will see you. Why don't you hide?"

"I'm looking at the pool down there. Isn't it beautiful?"

But Coyote said, "I don't see anything so special about it."

"Oh, it's very special," Fox told him. "It's sacred. Tonight there will be medicine in that pool."

Now Coyote was interested.

So Fox said, "Tonight Creator will put a big piece of sacred fry bread in that pool as an offering. Wait here with me. You will see."

So they waited together on the hill.

Just as the sun went down, the moon came up and suddenly a big piece of fry bread slid into the pool.

When Coyote saw it, he nearly fainted.

It was the biggest piece of fry bread he'd ever seen.

"I want that bread!" he said. "How can we get it?"

Fox said, "That's sacred fry bread! You can't eat it!"

"I'm hungry!" Coyote said. "I'm going to eat it! Show me how to get it."

"Don't be such a greedy fool! Creator might send you trouble instead of bread."

But Coyote insisted that he had to have that bread.

So Fox took him near the edge of the pool. From there Coyote could see the bread on the other side. It seemed to be getting larger.

"Now what do I do?" he asked excitedly.

"Just start drinking," Fox told him. "As you drink, you will draw it to you."

Then he sat back to watch. He tried not to laugh as Coyote drank and drank. While the pool got smaller and smaller, Coyote got bigger and bigger.

But he could see the bread getting closer and closer. At last it was close enough so he tried to grab it. Just then Fox threw a stone into the puddle and the bread turned into ripples and rings.

Then Coyote realized that he'd been tricked. He tried to chase Fox, but his belly was so full of water that he could not run.

"If you hadn't been so greedy, I couldn't have fooled you. But you let your belly rule your head again! Now you will suffer for trying to steal Creator's sacred fry bread."

Fox walked off laughing, while Coyote just sat and cried.

THE FIRST RAINBOW

One summer day when the wind was blowing gently over the prairie, the flowers began whispering together.

"Our families have been here many summers and next year our children will grow up here. They will give great beauty to the earth, as we are doing now," said a brown-eyed Susan.

The blue bell said, "Yes, but I'm thinking of the great white winter that is coming. How we will fade and die in the cold. Next year our children will grow and die, too."

"It would be so nice," said a violet, "if we got to go a happy place beyond earth."

"Let us ask Creator about that," said a tall goldenrod.

"But our voices will be too small," worried a blue aster. "Perhaps we could ask the little girl who comes to walk among us, if she will speak for us."

The child came almost daily, for she loved to sit among the flowers and watch them nod their bright heads in the summer breeze.

"Would you speak to Creator for us?" Tiger lily asked when the child came again. "Please tell Creator that we would like a place to go after we fade and die."

The little girl loved the flowers.

"I think that's a wonderful idea!" she exclaimed.

She wasn't certain that her voice would carry far enough. But she knew that Creator had many helpers.

It was Owl who heard her pray for the flowers. It was Owl who spoke to Creator in their behalf.

Then Owl spoke to the flowers, too. "It's done! When the thunder birds bring the last rain, look up into the sky. You will see the beauty of all the flowers who have ever lived on earth!"

Then when the summer was nearly over and the thunder birds arrived with the last rain... it happened. After it stopped raining, the clouds were streaked with light and the flowers looked up. Sure enough there in the sky was a great band of many beautiful flower colors.

Yes, it was the first rainbow!

ABOUT THE AUTHOR

Anne M. Dunn, Anishinabeg/Ojibwe grandmother and story-teller, is the author of two previous collections, *When Beaver Was Very Great* (Midwest Editions) and *Grandmother's Gift: Stories from the Anishinabeg* (Holy Cow! Press). With her mother, Maefred Arey, and daughter, Annette Humphrey Brien, she has produced a cassette collection of Anishinabe Grandmother Stories. Along with a community of artists from several nations, she produced a CD collection of stories and songs for the Whispering Tree Project. A world traveler and peace activist, she has recently visited Austria and Scotland, as well as Puget Sound, Washington, the Black Hills, and she covered over 4,000 miles with the Peace Caravan, to bring awareness about Chiapas, Mexico and raising humanitarian aide for Nicaragua. She has been a guest at the Norcroft-A Writing Retreat for Women in northern Minnesota and her plays have been performed at the Mesabi Children's Art Camp and the White Earth Art Camp. She lives on the Leech Lake reservation near Cass Lake, Minnesota.

ABOUT THE ARTIST

Cynthia Holmes is an enrolled member of the Minnesota Chippewa Tribe—Mississippi Band, White Earth. She began her career as a costumer for theatre and film but soon discovered a passion for painting and sculpting. Her tribal art forms, inclusive of jewelry and leather clothing have been exhibited internationally. She has been a costumer for the Guthrie and Children's Theatres in Minneapolis and an assistant designer for Warner Brothers production of Prince's "Purple Rain." She currently teaches art at Fond du Lac Tribal and Community College in Cloquet, Minnesota.